Life in abundance!

Irène Grosjean

Life in abundance!

Biovie

Eric Viard – Éditions Biovie
60 chemin des comminques
30980 Langlade
www.biovie.fr

Publishing supervisor
Aurélie Viard
www.aucoeurdelaconnaissance.info

Layout
Tech It – www.techitmadagascar.com

TECH IT

Front cover
Rudi Hartono

Back cover text
Dr Cyril Gacond: "I met Irène Grosjean 25 years ago when I worked as a practitioner doctor and when I specialized in nutrition.
Irène's approach had in that case drawn my attention because I never believed that chronic and metabolic diseases, particularly, "were a godsend" and I knew, according to my studies, that the biggest majority of the pathologies were not originally from genetics. Irène enabled me to expand my vision of therapeutic, and especially, preventive possibilities."

Introduction
Damien Artero, filmmaker: **Beyond its multiple hats, author, director, lecturer, animator and photographer, loving dad, it is really living food, which binds Damien Artero and Irène Grosjean.**
Friends, they share recipes, experiences and expertise about living food.
You can discover him, him and his work, on his website www.planeted.eu.

Inside photographies
Famille Grosjean, Aurélie et Eric Viard, Damien Artero
Le Chou Brave: www.lechoubrave.fr

Printing
For the printing of this book in PEFC-certified paper from sustainably managed forests (100% recycled paper was not available at the national level during the printing) and plant-based inks, Biovie has chosen the printing company Pure Impression located in Maugio in Hérault.
Pure Impression is the only printing company from France established in an HQE building owning 2000 m2 of photovoltaic roofing panels.
The rain waters are collected and recycled. The calories generated by the machines are collected to heat or cool down the production area.
99% of the solid and liquid waste are recycled.
The printing company is also committed at the social level: profit's sharing with the employees, identical salaries between men and women. The disabled staff form 12% of the employees.

www.pure-impression.fr

ISBN : 9782957319015

First edition legal submission: December 2018
Printing third edition April 2020: 30 000 copies
Total printing since December 2018: 50 000 copies

Table of content

Thanks

THANK YOU to all of my "boosters", so what I wrote more than 20 years ago can finally be published and

BRING SENSE BACK INTO THE WORLD...

...to as many unhappy or sick people as possible in any way... Because nature has given us everything to make each of us a healthy, creative, and happy being, a Co-Creator of the Universe; and not a sick, unhappy DESTRUCTOR of ONSELF and the UNIVERSE...

Two days before he left us, my husband said to me:

- *I am going to take away all your material worries so that you can do what you have to do...*
- *What do I have to do?*
- *You know what to do!* – He answered, and two days later he died.

So, if he was not the one who took them away from me, I could think that he had entrusted this mission to our son Philippe, whom I thank infinitely for having always happily taken this on... and who practically forced me to get my book out of his dungeons. So, THANK YOU, a thousand thanks Philippe and may life return to you a hundredfold what you so generously give out.

He is not the only one to have done so, and I also thank my eldest daughter Nelly who has created this wonderful "Musée des Arômes et du Parfum" (Museum of Aromas and Perfume) in Graveson en Provence and "Moulin de Vies" (Mill of Lifes) in Switzerland to promote TRUE, COMPLETE and NATURAL HEALTH. Her fabulous essential oils wonderfully contribute to protect, improve, and sometimes even restore health.

THANK YOU also, big THANK YOU to Sylvie who was an emergency doctor for 15 years and who said me one morning: "*I think I'm going to make you happy mom, I've registered at the naturopathy school*".
When she was four years old, she said to me: "*You know mom, it's not about making money, it's about sending a message...*"
Which she manages very well through the "Jardin de Vies" (Garden of Lives) that, she and Doug her husband, created in Flayosc, a wonderful village in Provence, where they're happy to welcome you for a beneficial and pleasant fasting or detoxification treatment.
Not to mention the amazing use of cupping that cure bronchopneumonia, pleurisy and pulmonary congestion of the

past centuries and which, thanks to a prodigious modern device, will help you to relieve yourself of all your painful and embarrassing problems such as bronchitis, asthma, anxiety, fears, sadness, dark thoughts etc...
So, THANK YOU also to Sylvie and Doug to whom I wish full success on their business!

How can I not also thank Elaine, the mother of my grand-children's, who is a pediatrician in Avignon and who does transitional work between symptomatic medicine and that of the root causes of all diseases... how precious and promising...

And how not to also thank my architect son, Jean-Lou, who is a builder of the most amazing schools that just make you want to be a student again...

Not forgetting Marilys, my artist daughter-in-law who embellishes everything she touches...

And also, how can I not thank them all for the beautiful place they offered me to live, when having lost the property, I loved and having neither husband nor children with me, I did not see the point of settling back comfortably...

So first of all, I will say THANK YOU to each of my children, grandchildren, and great-grandchildren and to those who accompany them, for their incredible support and encouragement.

A big thank you of course to Dr Cyril Gacond, thanks to whom will soon be created an earthly paradise in

Morocco, near Marrakech, comprising of a wonderful "Club Vacances Santé" (Health Holiday Club) enabling all those who wish to discover in a holiday setting, the joy of life, health and well-being.

THANK YOU to my precious secretary Marlyse, to her husband Antoine, to Jean-Charles, Michèle, Brigitte and Dr Miguel Barthéléry, who teach or have at one time taught the amazing team that allows me to do what I'm doing.

THANK YOU also to Alain and Gregory from Vidya Ayurveda who invited me to give lectures and workshops in Belgium.

THANK YOU, big thanks to Gilles, Georges, Yoyo, and all my friends, whom I consider as my children.

THANK YOU of course to my friend Raymond who initiated us first, to Mr. Pierre-Valentin Marchesseau, Damien Artero, Christophe Fender, Carine Phung and Yann Deva, who so brilliantly directed this wonderful video "La Vie en Abondance" that has been around the world (NDT: you may watch this video on YouTube with English subtitles).

THANK YOU, thank you, thank you, thank you again to all those who trusted me and allowed me to practice and confirm what I had partly learnt and partly was going to discover or rediscover...

For the laws of life are immutable and eternal, and nothing can abolish or change them...

...SO, THANK YOU, THANK YOU, THANK YOU FOR ALL THE HARDSHIPS THAT HAVE PUT ME BACK ON THEIR PATH...

THE RIGHT PATH, THAT OF LIFE AND ALL ITS BENEFITS, for which, I will never tire of saying it, nature has given us everything...

Irene Grosjean

Editor's foreword

You have *Life In Abundance* in your hands.

Our publishing adventure finishes here, and the book's odyssey starts now.

Because that is for sure, its path will be long and beautiful!

It will travel in many countries.

It will be determining for many of you.

We are grateful to have taken up the challenge, to have been chosen to publish the life experience of Irène Grosjean.

We took care to remain attentive, authentic and clear, in permanent connection with Irène to publish her message in the most accurate way possible.

It was fascinating and we are proud and happy to have been able to contribute this way, so that a so-precious knowledge is to be largely passed down.

What I remember from the first reading of this manuscript, is all the wisdom of this young lady of 90 years old, dynamic, sensitive and loving.

You will understand how to take care of your kids and help them to grow well, so that they are able, in their turn, to create their paradise.

You will learn from which health resources you have inherited, and you will have the keys to re-establish the harmony with your strengths and weaknesses.

You will be able to follow the path of love, of peace, of creativity, of abundance and faith, which, let's be honest, for most of us, are only abstract and utopian concepts!

What you are going to read will most probably affect you. Even maybe make yourself angry. You maybe will feel like defending vigorously what you have learned until today. But as the day follows the night, our emotions and our well fixed ideas don't change much, the fondamental laws of life are not negotiable!

The question you will have to answer is not whether if you liked this book or not, if it taught you something or not, but well and truly what is your choice.

Because our power and freedom are here.

To follow the intelligence of life or to continue to destroy ourselves?

My answer is: "yes, I choose life!"

Thank you for everything, dearest Irène.

Thank your for my kids, thank you for my friends, thank you for all this inspiration you offer me with generosity and thank you for your so delicious dishes.

Happy reading and bon voyage!

Aurélie Viard,
publishing supervisor

Preface

"*Let food be thy medicine*" Hippocrates taught.
When more and more questions arise in people's minds, such as the composition and quality of their food, joining Irene's table plunges you into a bath of vitality. And this is not only a figure of speech: as a certified naturopath, this dynamic young lady in her 90th year, dedicated her entire life to natural health and live food, combining amazing results with a colossal experience. "Alive" ... This is the first qualifying term that arises in mind when you spend some time with Irene. Her energy seems inexhaustible! Because she harvests it from its best and endless source: Nature.

The finest gourmets and the greatest food lovers will be fulfilled with the abundance of Irene's vegan and raw "cook" (NDT: that we call sometime in French "crusine"). Those of us that are fatigued will recover energy and performance, by implementing her naturopath's guidelines. In this enlightened book, brimming with flavor and enthusiasm, Irene synthesizes her medicinal know-how as well as her culinary skills. She places our nutrition back in its central, fundamental place, and shows us nothing less than how to master our wellbeing and health.

On the menu: Breathe, Eat, Sleep, Eliminate... To live being really alive!

Damien Artero: author, film director, lecturer, animator, photographer, loving father. And live raw food expert. You can discover him and his work on his website www.planeted.eu

Introduction

WHY
So much suffering, depravation, illnesses,
and wars in our world?

WHY
So much violence, rapes, and crimes?

WHY
Do so many young people take drugs or take
their own lives at the dawn of their existence?

WHY
Is one part of the world still starving while
the other is overfed?

WHY
Despite the progress of science, medicine,
and high technology, do we still need more hospitals,
psychiatric clinics, or penitentiaries?

WHY? WHY?

Perhaps did you ask yourself these questions that took me decades of research, studies and experience, to let me discover that all the suffering, all the diseases, all the misery, all the wars, all the madness and all the crimes of humanity have one and single cause....

Only one and single cause apparently of little importance, although so essential... Oh, I know that you might find it hard to believe me, still, I also know that everything in this world, like the functioning of our body, is ruled by laws, rules and principles that simple common sense asks us to respect, if we want that the cells which constitute our body, connect to the frequencies of life.

Frequencies which, by themselves, can provide us with a True, Complete and Natural Health. Without this, it is impossible to seize that happiness that we are searching for, while nature has already so simply, so truly given to us.

The body

To make our journey through life, as we come into this world, we receive a body that we will abandon at the terminus.

A body that we can compare to a vehicle which would have the power and qualities that are essential to our earthly mission.

A body carefully crafted, composed of different extremely sophisticated systems, all crucial to its functioning.

Whether they are bones, muscular, glandular, nervous, respiratory, digestive, circulatory, genital, cutaneous, pilous, etc. They are all composed of organs, glands, nerves, blood vessels, muscles, mucous membranes, bones etc. Themselves made of liquids, cells, that we one day discovered only after the invention of the electronic microscope.

For one third, our body is made of cells, while the two other thirds are liquids. That is to say 44 pounds (20 kg) of cells and 88 pounds (40 kg) of liquids for a 132 pounds (60 kg) body.

88 pounds of liquids are made of 170 us fl oz (5 liters) of blood and 1 183 us fl oz (35 liters) of interstitial liquids that our elders, who were maybe not scholars but who knew, used to call humors!

And finally, we are made of cells, who is smallest one measures, as it is said, one thousandth of a millimeter.

Almost unthinkable!

Especially if we consider that whether muscular, bones, blood, nervous, or cerebral, almost all these cells possess a respiratory, digestive, circulatory, reproductive system, as well as a brain containing a memory strip called DNA...

A brain that we might, although schematically, compare to an emission and receptor device, that not only allows it to communicate with other cells, in order to maintain our extraordinary living laboratory, but also, and this is prodigious, that contains the creative intelligence of these cells.

Therefore, the necessity, the extreme necessity to understand the functioning of our body and of the cells and liquids which it is made up of.

This is the reason why the sheer common sense would demand that we take the best care of our body. So that, tall or small, strong or weak, it finds its place in the great universal puzzle, where it can be the best companion, always ready to serve, if only we treat it as it deserves. Or it could behave as a tyrannical and demanding master if we fail to take care of it.

What are these laws?

Considering that that we come into this world and leave it with a breath, we could say that **the first law is breathe.**

Immediately after coming out of our mother's womb, we seek to feed from her breast. We can then say that **the second law is eat.**

And as we fall asleep once we have been breast-fed, so that we can digest this divine nectar which residue will be expelled when we wake up, **the third law is sleep** and **the fourth eliminate.**

Are these four basic laws always respected?

Our dear little cells will allow us to connect with the highest frequency they can reach. And it will be the highest and most creative one, as long as it is respected.

Then we will be able to love, think and act for our own good and that of others.

Whereas if one or another of these four laws is neglected, our dear little cells will only be able to tune up with the frequency that they can reach. Which will be as low, inverted, and destructive as the cells are poisoned and deficient.

Then we will have a life of suffering, fears, shortage, conflicts, and illnesses.

This is why it is so fundamental to remember and respect these 4 basic laws, that will make us a happy and co-creator of ourselves and of the Universe, if they are heeded...

Or a miserable wrecker of ourselves and of the Universe if they are not.

Love

These 4 basic laws will enable us to love, think and act for all our life.

To love thanks to the emotions that we sang, poetized, claimed, and proclaimed, on every level. Unless perhaps one wants the life that we have been given, to allow us to make choices, all the choices, to be happy or sad.

According to....
these 4 laws are respected or not

From our birth to our passing, don't we choose everything that concerns us according to what we like or do not like?

Whether it is food, drinks, relationships, activities, leisure, music, shapes, colors, temperature, climate, etc.

From his birth does not the baby prefer his mother's breast to the plastic teats that she forces him to suckle?

Does he or does not he eat chocolate, meat, sweet, salt, chips, pasta, or fruit...Because he likes it or not?

Once he is grown up will he listen to Mozart, Wagner, pop, folk, or classical music, again for the same reason?

Will he or not, wear white, blue, black, yellow, red, green or all the other colors, just because he does or does not like them?

Will he go on holidays to the mountains in Canada, or in Northern Europe if he enjoys the cold, or in the tropics if he likes the sun and warmth? Isn't it also true that he will choose his profession according to what he appreciates even if he has no guarantee that it works well?

Not to mention his or her companion who will be chosen for love.

Do animals like what they eat?

We ignore it.

Still we know that they eat what nature intended for their digestive system and the way it was built.

I am talking about wild animals of course. Not domesticated by man, who, similarly, have the sad privilege of needing doctors, to be more precise veterinarians, which is a fast-growing profession. I noticed recently whilst travelling through the Swiss countryside where even the tiniest village has its veterinary clinic.

Cats from my childhood were never sick... Fed with their hunt, the worse they had would be an indigestion, if the feast had been too rich. They were active and playful. Fed with cat food and kibble, our cats are not anymore.

Progress? For whom?

Do animals, like us, love their companion?

For a certain number we can think they do. One winter day, a pair of swans, sliding majestically over the Doubs River, arrived on the heart of Bief, a small village of France, where I used to live. Wonderfully white and graceful, they quickly became the children's center of attention. 6 months later, only one remained on the opposite shore. His partner had been shot by a cynical hunter.

To appease our sadness, the town council decided to offer a new female partner to the remaining swan. But he refused her. She was then changed for another one, then another. But he refused them all and continued to wander in solitude with dignity.

Everyone who loves animals knows a similar story showing that our friend's animals, are like us, sentient creatures. An offering from Life, driving us towards this happiness that we presume exists, and which, similarly, must adhere to certain rules.

I learnt through experience that joy and happiness are much easier to find when our body is at its best. And when it is not so, our dear little cells can only lead us to fleeting, painful and destructive passions.

This means that love is a pure emanation of soul because what else could let us love?

Love did I say, is for each one of us, the safest guide, when our cells work perfectly, and it is the worst misleading adviser if it is not so.

Indeed, as we will see further on, as soon as they are asphyxiated, deficient or poisoned, when they cannot rely on life's intelligence, our dear little cells start messing up.

Opposite to common sense,
the one that belongs to life
and all its beneficence.

The ideas

Consequently, we could say that if life offered us love to guide us in our choices, she also gave us the ideas to be informed throughout our existence.

The ideas spur into our head and so do feelings in our heart.

the ideas will be:

- **high**
- **clear**
- **wise**
- **precise**
- **joyful**
- **constructive**
- **straight**

If, as we have just seen for love and feelings, when the functioning of our body and cells is respected,

if not, they will be:

- **gloomy**
- **dark**
- **insane**
- **chaotic**
- **sad**
- **destructive**
- **twisted**

Wasn't it said that after they committed the original sin, Adam and Eva could not hear their Creator's voice, but a new voice never heard before? Wouldn't this, these voices, be the ideas that the creative intelligence uses to inform its creatures of everything they need to know for their earthly life?

Ideas that could be messengers from the universe!

Ideas which always showed up at times when we most needed them, sometimes in different parts of the world at the same moment. Like the idea of printing for example, which soared in Gutenberg's mind in Germany, when it was identically discovered in China at the same time.

Ideas that seem to get to us only once we are able to implement them. What would Charlemagne have done with the idea of building a nuclear power plant?

Could ideas, just like tv or radio programs, be sent by a transmitter and caught by a receiver?

Simply looking at a brain cell helps you imagine it. Like the most sophisticated antennas, their dendrites stretch to all directions and seize the ideas that they tell the brain.

Who knows if one should memorize them, throw them away or change them into decisions and take, or not take action?

Ideas, as my 60 years of experience allow me to think, could be conveyed on a particular and precise wavelength.

Because as we know it today, everything is made of wavelengths or frequencies!

Heading to the conclusion that our brain and nervous cells could be a sort of terminal for the great cosmic computer, is just a step away.

Which would mean that we did not create anything. This prodigious system, that reciprocally links the creature and its creator, could perfectly be the first and most prestigious computer of all. In this system, some brains would have the privilege to copy, thanks to the "ideas", what their cells have captured.

This system called Spirit, that is said to be "divine" or "from life", when our dear little cells are able to reach the highest frequency. This frequency conveys ideas that are all the clearer, more precise, and more constructive, the more our cells are well oxygenated, well-nourished and bathed in an environment that is at least clean, if not pure. Some ideas could be qualified insane or devilish when our cells are weakened, asphyxiated, deficient or poisoned. They can only rely on the frequency they can reach, which is the lowest one.

Some centuries ago, speaking this language would probably have led me to the stake, burnt by the Inquisition. Since then, science has discovered the infinite world of wavelength frequencies and created quantities of devices to receive and emit such waves. It is not possible to deny the analogies that exist between the means of communication that life provides us, with the television, telephone, radio, or computer services which have extensively developed.

The first of these analogies is that, just as it is not possible to listen to the radio or watch TV without a device,

It is not possible to produce feelings or receive ideas, without the body and the cells that compose it.

The second one is that, just as the sound quality of a radio broadcasting depends on the quality of the radio that receives or sends it,

The clarity of our feelings and ideas also depends on the quality and proper functioning of our dear little cells.

In other words, like a radio or quality TV is able to receive the best programs, a low-quality device will only be able to connect to mediocre programs.

These two elements are probably the starting point of what made people become either geniuses or idiots.

The third analogy: like a black and white TV cannot play a colored image,

Whatever we try, our cells will never be able to receive ideas for which they were not designed.

A reason why a mathematician is interested in mathematics when a philosopher deals with philosophy.

From this analogy, thinking that the highest and most constructive ideas are spread by the life intelligence, is just another step away, that the practice of natural methods have led me to take.

And as one recognizes a tree from its fruit, I did not hesitate to go to the conclusion that the highest ideas belong to life that religions usually qualify as divine or spiritual.

And that the lowest and destructive ideas are produced by the inverted intelligence, called insane, demonic, or devilish.

The life intelligence being the one that certain religions call God, while the inverted and destructive intelligence is called Devil.

We understand that this first possibility seems to take us to our own highest destiny, as well as to the global one. And the second leads us to all the suffering or possible horrors.

It might be the reason why, since the dawn of time our body has formed, with our soul and spirit, this indivisible trinity aimed to guide us.

To make our lives a paradise of wellness, joy, love, peace, creativity, prosperity, which the universal intelligence has given.

Or a hell of adversity, fears, sadness, conflicts, wars, diseases, and frustrations that the non-respect of the natural basic laws allow us to create.

Nutrition

This is the reason why we are going to look more specifically at our body, this astonishing laboratory of life, and at the four basic laws with which it operates. We will not start with the first law, breathing, that we will see later, but with

Nutrition, because this one seems to be the less respected.

A kind of nutrition that will not refer to some famous expert theories, but to the "common sense". It will guide us to determine which fuel our maker – called Creator – designed for us.

One day, as I was attending a workshop on edible plants, I started to conscientiously chew this plant that resembled a fake carrot that neither tasted of fennel nor aniseed although the plant resembled it. I suddenly sensed a revulsion that forced me to spit out what was in my mouth.

At the same time, a participant to whom I had lent a book to recognize plants, yelled "*this is poison hemlock!*". And it was truly a sort of long hemlock that, with all its strength, my body had refused to let me swallow. Once again, I was amazed by this life intelligence that permanently intervenes to protect us.

I said to myself that if I had not chewed as I did, I would have finally swallowed it. Like wild animals, this is probably how our ancestors, the first human beings, discovered their food.

You probably learnt like I did in school, that the digestive tract of pigs is the closest to ours, and similarly to it, we are omnivores.

Later, when I discovered the hypothesis of the biologist Pierre-Valentin Marchesseau, who highlights the analogies between man's digestive tract and that of great apes, I felt more comfortable.

Especially when I learnt that, like women, female monkeys, gorillas, chimps, and orangutans had periods every moon and carried their babies nine moons before they were born.

Is it maybe one of the reasons why scientists said that we come from apes? But this is another story, because if so, apes should have disappeared... But let us go back to nutrition.

Like all species, we should be able to feed ourselves only with the means provided by our body.

Are we like animals (word meaning that we must animate to get our food), able to catch and kill a rabbit, a hare, a wild boar, a bird or a living fish, bite through its skin and fur, its feathers or scales, to enjoy its flesh and guts, while, still warm, its blood is pouring into our mouth? Doe this makes you shiver? Me too!

This feeling proves that we are not the carnivore that we pretend we are.

Because if so, we could kill our prey and eat it the same way.

~ ***So, if we are not carnivore, maybe we should eat grass from the fields?*** ~

But since we do not have the digestive system of an herbivore, capable to ruminate and digest the thick cellulose of hay and grass, it is unlikely that we were designed for it.

~ ***If we are neither carnivore nor herbivores, are we perhaps granivores?*** ~

In that case, like all granivores on earth we should have a beak to peck and a gizzard to digest... But as we do not have these, we probably cannot be fed on grain.

~ ***So, what is our food?*** ~

Didn't we learn that the first humans were gatherers and thousands of years later, they became hunters?

~ ***For what reason?*** ~

This is the main question that we should ask ourselves. We have all heard of the continent of Atlantis that sank into the ocean... Also, of the separation of Africa and South America... It is then easy to understand that these events created a tremendous shock to the earth, which could have had a ripple effect.

Except under the tropics and the equator, which remained basked in sunshine, the earth had regions yielding less fruit.

And moreover, experiencing cold weather, humans discovered how to make fire and cooked the leaves and roots which replaced the fruit that the colder earth could not provide anymore.

But as this cooked and dead food was not sufficient, they had to kill animal to get their energy.

But here is the thing. As humans did not have the digestive system of a carnivore, feeding off this cooked and meaty food, they began their descent to hell.

The first time I heard the founder of the Naturopathic College say that cooking food had been the worst error of mankind, the first sin in some ways, that gradually engendered all the illnesses, I was rather doubtful. But after 60 years of practice and experience, I can say that today I totally agree with this idea.

Because the truth is determined through facts, ever repeated. This simple truth that one cannot deny, even

though some still say that that it does not exist and that looking for it is pointless.

"*Listen little one*", once said my father, on a spring morning, listening to the birds.

"*Since the beginning of the world, their song is still as beautiful, whereas most music and songs that once have been popular, soon go out of fashion. Remember,* ***what is true is never out of date.***"

A wise saying that I am happy to share with you.

Why should it be different with cooked food which has always been and remains dead?

Whereas a raw plant food that corresponds to our digestive system is always filled with the energy of soil, air, water, and sun. In other words, filled with life, for it is its mission to pass it onto us.

Who could pretend that cooking does not remove this subtle and indivisible energy from food, that is called life?

Do you know any farmer who would have this strange idea to cook his grain before he sows it? Or a countrywoman who would boil her eggs before she has them brooded?

Of course not!

One and the other perfectly know that cooked grain will never sprout or that the hen who received boiled eggs will wait forever before she sees her chicks.

Still is not it what we do every day, when we cook, grill, sterilize, pasteurize, simmer, or ferment our food?

All of this, without ever asking ourselves how will a cooked nutrient, transmit the energy of the sun, the water, the air, the soil or in other words the life that heating has taken away.

This energy which is for our life what fuel is for the car engine, or electricity for the device. This energy that is essential to live.

Curious and full of good sense, the founder of the Naturopathic College, one day brought his eggs to a laboratory for analysis. One was raw and the other one boiled. To his great surprise he received the same results for both.

Would science have forgotten what life is?

It is true, the author Antoine de Saint Exupery said, that "*what is essential is invisible for the eyes*".

In order to get his students to perfectly understand, Pierre-Valentin Marchesseau used to say:

"*Imagine that, parked in front of your house, there are two cars. In the first one the driver is alive and in the second one he is dead. Which car will you chose?*" That makes its own case.

By the way, what is a living element?

By definition it is an element that is animated by the life intelligence. Following what, it is born, grows, strengthens, then dies, decomposes, and gives back its elements to the soil, that will absorb, transform, and use it, so that life continues.

***"Nothing is lost, nothing is created, everything is transformed!"* said the famous chemist Lavoisier.**

The products created by the reverse intelligence have always been and will forever be unable to incorporate into the eternal process of life and can only disturb it.

I was thinking, the other day while sweeping the dead leaves in my garden, that they are never a nuisance to the forest, where they nicely lay in a heap under the trees. They will turn into humus that decomposes, nourishing other trees, dropping their leaves, and so on until the end of time.

Isn't it so with every living thing, that participates to the beauty and harmony, to the continuum of life?

This reminds me of a story that I was telling my grand-son one day, as he passed me by with a chocolate bar in his hand, carefully hidden behind his back. Calling him I told him this story...

"When the earth was created, his founder had planned everything for people to love one another, to be healthy, happy, beautiful, and creative, for their own good and that of everyone...

But on Earth, nature was not alone. A little devil had slipped in it. He did not want nature to win, nor humans to love or be beautiful, happy, and healthy…

No! He wanted them to be ugly and distorted. He wanted them to suffer and be sick, to fight and even kill one another in all sorts of ways."

"*Oh! And how did he do?*" asked my little boy

"*How did he do? It is very simple: everything that nature gave to us is alive. And we can only create life with what is alive. A really happy and fulfilled life. Whereas, everything that the devil gave them, is dead. And death can only produce death, misfortune and sickness."*

With these words Sebastian walked back, his hand still behind his back, and then came back holding an apple.

"*Well done little one! You got it! Because if you plant an apple you will get an apple tree which, in time, will give you apples which in their turn will make apple trees…*

And if you plant your chocolate bar, or as many chocolate bars as you want, you will never get a chocolate field… Because it is dead, and we cannot create life from death."

Later one, Sebastien ranged me and said: "*Granny, tell Sylvain, because he doesn't believe me. Tell him that candies are dead and that it's not good."*

One day, I attended a presentation as I wanted to know if the vitamins used in a laboratory for natural products were natural vitamins or synthetic molecules. Then I asked my question to the Doctor who was boasting the merits of his drugs. After asking three times he finally answered:

"Madam, everyone knows that a molecule is a molecule, whether it is synthetic or natural. It is equivalent."

How can someone think such a thing?

Even if the death of living beings seems to be an indispensable step to their necessary transformation, leading to evolution, synthetic elements, created out of nowhere with combinations that are foreign to Life, are not recyclable. Just like this plastic bag that will never grow even if we stick it in the best soil. It will never be able to decompose and will only invade, smirch, and disrupt the universal order to which it does not belong.

This drives to the "pollution" that surrounds us in the most worrying way.

Unlike the leaves which only use the life elements that they have drawn from the air, the soil, the sun, and the water, to provide us with their shade and chlorophyll.

How could human beings forget this invisible, unanalyzable something called Life? We only realize its value and consider how precious it is, once we are about to lose it.

Life is indivisible from the food that fuels it.

Because according to our unshakeable habits, whales or penguins in the North Pole should cook their food and eat hot plates to warm up. Why don't they?

Because their instinct knows that heating food will destroy the energy that they need.

Like the author, Mr. Edmond Bordeaux Szekely says in this passage taken from the Dead Sea Scrolls:

> Someone asked me
>
> *"Master, where is the life bonfire?*
>
> *In you, in your blood and your body"*
>
> Others asked:
>
> *"Where is the fire of death?"*
>
> *"It is the fire that burnt out of your body and is hotter than your blood. With this fire you cook food in your homes. Truly I say to you it is the same fire of mischief that ravages your thoughts and destroys your spirit.*
>
> *Your body is what you eat, your spirit is what you think.*
>
> *Do not ever take anything that was killed by a hotter fire than the fire of life.*
>
> *Eat all the fruit from the trees that grow and ripen from the fire of life, and which are a gift from our mother earth. But never eat any of these nutrients that get their taste from the fire of death, because they are from Satan."*

Here is what my dear friend Simone recently told me. The famous nativity figures' maker. She was amazed by the prodigious transformations that occurred in her since we met, almost 15 years ago.

"At the age of 90, I did not feel the cold this winter, nor the fatigue. Although I worked more than usual. Since I have started eating raw food, I really feel like I'm getting younger."

"***Talk about rejuvenating Mrs. Grosjean, talk about it*****!** She said.
Simone is an example, among others. An example that shows how the illusion of cooked food is significant. I remember this winter Sundays at the Ballon d'Alsace, a mountain in France, where, with my husband and children, we ate our apples, nuts, and dates, in a preserved little corner, rather than in the noisy and smoky atmosphere of the chalet. And we could also ski on the deserted slopes during the best hours of the day.

Feel cold? Not us!

One day, the famous Dr. Kousmine, who was in charge of the cancerization of mice for a medical experiment, realized that the mice she fed with raw grains were totally resistant to cancer, whereas the mice fed with grilled grain were infected.

> ***Being a Doctor with high consciousness, she disclosed her discovery and pointed out the importance of raw food.***

Alas, like Durville, Rouhet, Marchesseau, Knapp, Geffroy, Mono, Khune, Carton, Shelton, Solomidès, Lagarde, Burger, Beljanski,... and other famous and inspired persons, who have worked to protect human's health and improve his condition, she had tremendous difficulties spreading her ideas, probably inspired by higher spheres, in a wheeler-dealer's world.

Why be inspired by lower ideas?

We will discuss this notion later. For now, let us consider a world fed with dead food, which had to replace the missing life-energy with stimulants.

Cooked and exciting foods that is the most common diet to civilized populations.

To clearly understand what exciting food is, let us imagine that we have two exhausted horses.

We give water, oats, and a nice litter to the first horse, so that eating and sleeping, our horse will reconstitute his energy to run again.

To the second one, we do not give any water nor food, but demand that he runs again at once.

How is he going to do, if not under our blows, forcing him to walk, urged by pain, and drawing on his glandular reserves to get some energy?

How many times will he be able to run again? 5, 6, 10, 20 times?

This question can only be answered by the energy reserves that he possesses. And once they are drained the horse will fall dead.

It is exactly similar with the cooked foods and the energizers such as meat, tea, coffee, sweet treats, and alcohol, that we consume. If they provide some euphoria for a short time, we can only be dependent on them as they give us less and less of this euphoria.

Same with drugs, that persons fed with live, energetic food, will never need.

Once again, let us consider the necessity to feed our children correctly. So that they never need these drugs, which can bring them nothing but some ephemeral fake euphoria.

That makes perfect sense!

I recently met a bank Director who asked me how I felt about coffee. As an answer, I asked him what his opinion on uncovered cheques was. He smiled and I saw that he had understood me. Because, whatever these stimulants may be, they are nothing but an uncovered response leading to a more important energetic shortage. A source of stress and later on, of depression.

Excitation = Depression!

Since we are talking about food, let us look at the small mammals who, barely out of the womb, their eyes still closed, are searching for their mum's teats.

Except for human babies who see the divine nectar of their mother's breast, convinced by "progress", replaced in good conscience, with cow's milk. Although the life intelligence seemed to have especially elaborated this beverage for calves, isn't that right? Not only for their physical but also their mental and psychological needs, which do not have much to see with that of our offspring!

During the last century, the brand new dairy industry, willing to promote the commerce of milk, educated us, little girls, so that once we would be mothers, we would give up this ancestral habit to breast feed our babies. Replacing it with cow's milk, which was said to have all the best advantages.

I still remember my beloved schoolteacher repeating that not only was the cow's milk baby bottle more hygienic, but also more convenient, as anyone else could feed the baby, giving more free time to the mother. This was without realizing that both the mother and the baby could later on, miss these tender moments. To end her demonstration, my teacher pointed out that giving baby bottles with cow's milk to our babies, would prevent from sagging and misshapen breast.

If I had always taken her words for granted, this time I could not.

As we know, when their teeth grow, the digestives secretions of calves' change, in order to adapt to the digestion of grass and hay that they eat as adults. And from then, they cannot digest their mother's milk anymore, who, actually, stops producing it.

These unfortunate cows have been transformed into milk factories. We have been convinced that cow's milk and dairy products were for us humans, and endless source of calcium.

And the recent glory of science made us trust this.

Still, we have forgotten that milk digestion cannot be optimized for human babies and even less for adults, whose digestive secretions change.

This milk, so rich in calcium, becomes an acid solution that destroys and burns all our minerals and acts as the greatest demineralizing and decalcifying agent ever.

You do not believe me? Just ask people suffering of arthritis and rheumatism what they eat. You will see that they are fond of cheese and dairy products, for their pretended calcium interest of course!
This is why among all these supposed truths, it is essential to search for the real convenient food that keeps us healthy.

This food that will allow us to be healthy and creative, is the one that nature intended for our **digestive system and avoid the misery that oppresses us when it is wrong.**

Toxins and deficiencies

All the books referring to the first human beings, commonly say that, until they discovered fire, they fed with plant gathering.

Fire considered as a gift from God, warmed up the tribes, protected them from wild animals, but also lead to unforeseen consequences on their future.

Because cooking their food, they were deprived of the energy coming from the earth, the air, the sun, and the water. In other words, lacking the life that they should have received, they needed to consume nutrients that did not correspond to their system.

Like animal's flesh, that they started to hunt and eat, not realizing that, different from carnivores', their urinary tract could not filter and eliminate the uric acid produced by meat proteins.

And with this poisonous and poisoned food, they started to create the violence and the anger which became the bed of all wars and human crimes, and also of painful illnesses.

Almost nothing!

Moreover, with this fire that I am tempted to call a "fire of hell", they started to invent all sorts of soups, slops and hotpots of legumes and starch. Still not realizing that their liver and digestive secretions, normally designed to process fruit, could not completely digest these sugars, that far far later, they named "slow sugar", leaving in their guts a kind of slimy, mucoid substance.

This fire not only stood as the origin of all their disturbances, fears, shyness, and anguish, but also for their annoying, embarrassing though not painful diseases.

Do you think I am exaggerating?

I can understand. But after 60 years of practice in health and human happiness, I have learnt that, unbelievable as it may seem, the starting point of all our pains, sicknesses, wars, frustrations and diversions, all come from cooking food.

This is from this common and rather small mistake, that our cells, lacking vital energy, started to insidiously and certainly, connect to the low and destructive frequencies that the asphyxiated, deficient, and poisoned cells can only reach.

Guided and informed by states of consciousness and ideas that are conveyed by low frequencies and illusions, fear, and anger, we started to slip into an infernal spiral. Our heart, head and body started to make of our lives this suffering hell of frustrations, illnesses and misery leading to wars.

And moreover, to counteract this low energy cooked food, we started to consume more and more stimulants as a replacement.

Our body, always more and more deprived and poisoned, cannot eliminate this tremendous amount of residues in feces or urines. Thus, it gets forced to reduce and lyophilize them, to store them up in its liquids.

These liquids that our ancestors – who were not scientists the way we understand it now, but estimable observers – called "humors"!

Like they probably did, we can now observe that if we are correctly fed and rested, we are in a better humor than when we are tired or over fed.

This expresses the fundamental importance of a proper physiology, from which automatically depend our state of consciousness, our feelings, and ideas, all originating from our psychological, intellectual, emotional, and spiritual behavior.

They will be as elevated, happy, and constructive, as the quality and functioning of our cells are consistent with nature's plan.

Is it still necessary to remind all that cows would never have become sick if they had only been fed with grass and hay, which nature had designed for their digestive system?

And similarly, humans would never have become what they are if they had only eaten what they were made for.

It is as simple as that!

So, to achieve this simple goal, we should have followed the 4 basic functioning laws, that are, breathe, eat, sleep, and eliminate. And cooking food does not allow it.

Because as I said, when our cells are deficient, poisoned, and asphyxiated, they are unable to reach the high frequencies of life.

In such conditions, all they can reach is the inverted intelligence that pushes them to love nutrients that create the poison in which they bathe.

Turning us into food addicts, who eat and enjoy the poisonous nourishment where they live.

This misconception has made us forget our instinct, under the low frequencies of fear and ignorance. We replaced it with the intellect. It is certainly a great means to achieve very interesting things, but we have used it to create a hell of suffering, of wars and illnesses.

Small causes - big effects

The residues coming from nutrients that do not correspond to our digestive system, are a great danger to our health.

Just as nuclear waste is for the planet.

Because these residues not only alter our physical functions, but also our psychological, intellectual, and emotional condition.

This is why fast, and abstinence were prescribed by most religions, supposed to raise the spiritual level of their believers. So was water and brown bread for feeding the prisoners. A kind of semi-fasting which, by helping the cells' liquids cleanliness, might help them to access higher states of consciousness.

It amounts to saying that in order to have a happy heart, clear and creative ideas, as well as the energy to achieve them, we must start by helping our extraordinary laboratory of a body to love, think and act as intended by nature.

That is to say to provide it with nutrients planned by nature and the manner it was predicted. Which are raw food and plants.

Considering that our digestive system is similar to that of great apes, with the same engine same fuel, does it mean that our food should be identical?

What do great apes like chimps, gorillas and orangutans, whose female bear their babies nine moons and have periods every moon, eat?

Simply gathered plants that they do not cook.

Didn't we say that the first humans were gatherers?

But later turned into hunter-gatherers.

So why this transformation?

Firstly, to be gatherers, the planet Earth had to provide them with enough to gather all year long, like in the tropics where trees grow quantities of delicious fruit...

So, if they became hunters it is because they didn't have enough fruit to pick.

We could think that when the Atlantis was drowned under the sea while Africa separated from South America, it may have tumbled the planet that had less sun and could not offer as much fruit, humans' basic nutrient.

Discovering cold weather, human beings also discovered how to cook food

Since this food was not energetic enough, they started to kill animals, in order to get their energy. But since they did not have a carnivore digestive system, they could not evacuate the acid produced by meat, and they stored it in their "humors".

And it was the start of the disconnection from their instinct and from the cosmic levels.

It was the start of their descent to hell.

How not to think of E. Bordeaux Szekely, a researcher, who in 1945, found in the archives of the Vatican, manuscripts from the Essenes, who were living two thousand years ago and influenced the genesis of Christianism.

Appealed by this amazing knowledge he wrote many books including:

The Essene Gospels, where he explains that the Church suppressed them because they did not correspond to Her wishes.

"Thou shall not kill" said Jesus, *"because life was given by God, and what God gave, man cannot take back."*

"Truly I say to you this is from a unique mother that everything was born on earth. This is why he who kills, kills his brother. Away from this criminal, the terrestrial mother will turn, and his angels will flee."

"Truly I say to you, he who kills, takes his own life, and he who eats the flesh of slaughtered animals, eat the body of death."

"In its blood, each drop of their blood turns into poison, their breath becomes fetid, in its flesh their flesh becomes a purulent abscess, in its guts their guts putrefy..."

After this essential revelation, Jesus continued and said:

"Do not kill any human nor animal and don't destroy the food that you put into your mouth,

because if you eat living food, it will vivify you, but if you kill to get your food, the flesh of the slaughtered animals will be your death...

because life comes from life and death comes from death."

And Jesus continued:

"Do not cook anything with a fire hotter than the fire of life, or Satan will possess your being.

Because all that kills your food, also kills your body, kills your soul and your spirit."

But in the fourth century, the Council of Nicaea suppressed from the Bible a great number of texts that did not cope with the dogma of the Church. So, the peaceful message of harmony of the Essene almost totally disappeared from the Christian translations... So did the only true human vegetarian and live diet.

Could we imagine what would man's evolution have become if, instead of choosing to conceal and keep this teaching, the Church had spread it?

The die is cast

Since from there and in good conscience, we started to eat food that became more and more exciting, fake and dead, which slowly but certainly attracted us into an infernal spiral, where in the greatest illusion, we replaced the real treasures of life by those of the inverted intelligence.

It created all our deviations, depravations, declines...

It drowned us into a sort of dehumanization and transformed

- Our faith once able to move mountains,
  into paralyzing fears
- Our courage into cowardice
- Our love into hatred
- Our happiness into sadness
- Our tenderness into violence
- Our forgiveness into revenge
- Our wellbeing into discontent

- Our peace into wars
- Our beauty into ugliness
- Our sobriety into orgies
- And our beautiful health into sickness

As we could not open the doors of this terrible and gloomy realm, or blinded and unable to recognize truth from falsehood, we replaced the marvelous wonders of life by illusion. Leading to our self, life, and happiness destruction.

We also lost access to the universal conscious, and without the least compunction, we accomplished vile and inhuman acts.

We lost the mission plan that life had entrusted to us, to make our lives this “paradise” provided for all beings of the creation. **So, not remembering what we were here for, we started to do business!**

Not to improve the common good as well as ours, but to the detriment of our human brothers, exploiting their weaknesses to ensure our superiority. We harshly defended it with the blood and tears of the weakest, enslaving them, and letting them call us “lord”.

Time after time, we dismissed the God of life, love and abundance and changed him for power, glory and wealth that promised us to be almighty.

We misspent the earth’s resources to produce more and more useless or deleterious things. With these profits we could acquire everything we wanted, even people.

And we associated with others like us, believing in our superiority, authorizing us to shamelessly cheat, to acquire power, glory, trials, and wars and build our empire of illusions.

> ***Its loyal demons are, in reality, the tools of the inverted world.***

These demons never ceased to persuade us that, with them, we would be always stronger, always richer and admired. **We would become more powerful than with this poor, old and obsolete God. Even with the most sophisticated devices he allowed us to build, he was still invisible, so we could deny his very existence.**

As an ultimate paradox, we could build such creations and products that can only offer what they have. Dead molecules, unable to reproduce, foreign to the life process that they only dangerously disturb or impede.

But this was not a problem, because if they could destroy the water, the atmosphere, or the soil and also animals, plants and humans' lives, these products were much more profitable than natural goods. We forgot them simply because, disconnected from the universal intelligence, we elected the great profitability as our absolute master.

Which allows us to do every and anything, whether it is profitable.

We even made legal or honorable, to destroy our lives or that of the earth. We jeopardize our children's future, without paying attention while they grow up. And they turn to drug addictions, unemployment, or they even join a sect or take their own lives.

And for the remaining people, after this awful massacre, there will be toxic air, polluted water, synthetic products, to feed or cure them when they are sick.

If ever we can reach that moment without having destroyed a part of our planet with nukes and bacteria, that we created to preserve our economy.

And this is without counting with the illnesses skillfully and cunningly maintained, because they represent a lucrative market. But we forgot that one day they could backfire on us. And then even our money or our connections, could do nothing against a heart attack, cancer, drugs or AIDS of our sons, against our spouse desertion, his or her alcoholism, or the cystic fibrosis and myopathy of our grand-children reminding us: maybe you forgot a little thing...

Life
With the laws and principles, whatever you call them, that rule her!

Life is simple!

In regard of the ever-growing expanse of our diseases and miseries, we created a new medicine. A medicine that suppresses them, never trying to correct or search for their origin.

A medicine with a philosophy of local diagnostic and specific remedy, becoming only symptomatic and allopathic. It replaced the physiological and holistic medicine that existed on all continents and was passed from generation to generation, whether in Africa, in America, in Asia or in Europe.

A very expert medicine, that, just like the tree hides the forest, would get lost in detail and forget the essential: **health!**

Even if in the teachings of Rama in the traditional India, Hermes in Egypt, Zoroaster in Iran, Apollo in Greece, it is said that:

Any medical intervention should be done at the Total Being level, and not on his local disturbances. And the role

of a sincere medicine is not only to heal the disease, but to teach health.

I often say, and I am proud of it, that I lose my patients as soon as I find them. because once they have learnt to live and take care of themselves, they do not need me or anyone else anymore.

Let us remember that in the Antique China's time, when health was the most precious gift, the doctor was paid to keep the villagers healthy. And when they became ill, he had to heal them for free.

Wasn't it the golden age of China?

Under the aura of science and progress the medical college teaches the new doctor how to put a name on each symptom, when a patient suffers, or more precisely when his body calls for help. This body, urging for help to eliminate these residues that inappropriate feeding introduced in it.

He learns how to prescribe an examination or some drugs and operation that will conceal and stop this urging call, without ever asking himself what the origin of this sickness is, and how to modify it.

Even if Hippocrates, the great master, father of medicine, told his patients, some 2000 years ago:

"Let food be thy medicine"

He asked doctors to "*cure without damage*"!
These two elements have not changed since that time, although our very expert medical practice seems to have forgotten them. Because since the beginning of our world, our body, this prodigious laboratory, always searching for its perfect balance, has always functioned the same way.

This means that each time our body receives more energy than necessary for its daily operations, or when it is shocked and requires a lot of energy, **it does everything possible to get rid of this discomfort.**

As you have understood, this discomfort is made by the anti-natural accumulation of food residues that he could not eliminate in the feces and daily urine. Our body had to reduce and lyophilize them, then keep them in some "underground layers". In other words, it kept them in the cells' liquids where they bathe, and will have to release them, turning them back into their original form, in order to guide them through the best elimination way. This will be the intestinal path for the mucus and viscosities, and the kidney way for acid residues. This liberating operation requires an important quantity of energy, so we might feel tired, even very tired, when it happens.

Do we have a solid constitution and a lot of energy?

We will be in a great intestinal mess with the annoying and embarrassing diarrhea liberating us from the mucus and viscosities and suffer from a burning and painful urinary infection meant to eliminate the acid residues. Most of the time both will affect us, taking advantage of that opportunity to throw away everything that disturbs.

Do we have the great privilege to be connected to the life frequencies?

And have we kept our instinct?

Like a wild animal, we will go on a diet and rest until our body is freed from its poisoned overload, allowing us to recover our health and well-being condition.

Or have we lost this immense privilege?

Influenced by fear and ignoring the laws of life to which we are definitely tied, **we will qualify these elimination crises as illnesses, which, like the ancient Japanese said, are *"healing crises"*. And we will try to suppress them quickly.**

All this without realizing that we are not ill by chance, or because of a microbe, a virus, a cold or heat, any shock or other visible reason.

But because we are in *"dis-order"*. That means we disobeyed God's and Life's Orders. If we remember and obey these laws, we can recover simply by joyfully healing, laughing as healthy people do.

Whereas under the influence of fear and illusions coming from low and inverted frequencies, we can only try to stop these healing crises, without realizing that doing so, we stop our body from eliminating its residues, driving them back into the depth of our cells.

Being more and more intoxicated, they will cry for more poison, asking for the products in which they live. So, like a food addict, we will love and consume what hurts the most.

This infernal trap ties us to frequencies as low and inverted as our dear little cells are deficient and intoxicated.

But if we understand the wonderful role of these elimination crises that we take for disease, and if we help our body achieve them, we will soon recover our healthy and happy condition and will automatically be connected to the life frequencies, that are made of joy, happiness and creativity.

It is as simple as that because life is simple!

Only the devil, or what we called so, complicated things, to confuse mankind. He was not named the "malevolent" for no reason, but because that what he is.

Medicines

This is how, leaving the cosmic and universal guidance that had given us everything to make a paradise of our lives, we created suffering, misery, and wars, and all the diseases that turned our existence into hell.

I know that it may seem crazy or utopian to pretend that our conflicts, wars, shortages, and sicknesses, are all due to our dietary mistakes and to the toxemia that they engender. You will understand if you practice. I have often been told:

There is much more that diet

And it is true, I admit it

But if there are many other things, first comes our diet.

Because without the deficiencies and residues issued from our diet when it is not the way nature decided for us, these things would not exist.

Have a quick look at the French history, when the kings and nobles could afford to eat meat and drink wine, while the common people were fed with flour and starches.

Weren't the first ones, warriors, and dominators, while the poor people remained exploited al will?

And as we will see later, the nobles had to wear wigs to hide their hair, burned by the acids that their meat-based diet produced, and that human kidneys are unable to purge. Although their organism was struggling to get rid of them, mainly through a rescue path: their skin. So instead of bringing the appropriate minerals that they needed, their acidic blood burned their hair roots which finally fell. In the meantime, the common people fed with flour, kept them longer.

Do we love meat, ham, and delis?

Or do we prefer dairy products, and cheese?

In either case, we are likely to have an acidic residual overload that our kidneys, which are not carnivore kidneys, are not able to eliminate through our urine.

This attitude will force our body to store theses poisonous overloads in its liquids where they will destroy and burn the minerals that they touch. Leading to the loss of hair that great meat-eaters experience, without counting the wrath and violence engendered by an excess of acid in the nervous and cerebral system. Just like too much electricity in the air will cause storms.

The blood of common people fed with mush and starch, and therefore loaded with mucus, will only be able to slow down its cell functioning.

This transformation from liquid to solid state, reveals their acidic nature, which, by burning our nerve endings, provokes pain, all the pains that we experience.

This means, and I draw your attention to the fact that, each time we feel this pain somewhere, without being hurt by some shock, it means that our body is leading these tiny crystals from a solid to a liquid state, so that our kidneys can eliminate them in the urine or perspiration.

And whatever painful this transformation may be, we should not worry but rather rejoice!

On condition that, as you will learn further, we understand and help our body in this liberating mission.

Let us remember that, in addition to creating pain, the melting of these little crystals can also raise our body heat and provoke fever.

Fever, like all pains, is actually a liberating process that our organism uses to get rid of its poisoned overload.

Do we prefer bread, pasta, pizzas, potatoes, and starch?

Our residual surcharge will be made of mucus and phlegm, so we will call it "colloidal".

You have to understand that just like the dry rice sticking to the pan should firstly swell to detach, these viscosities and glues that dry up in our underground layers, should also take back their original shape to peel off and leave from where they are stored.

This liberating process requires a lot of energy, so we could be tired or very tired or even sick and hoarse or feel anxious and suffocate (asthma and emphysema). We could suffer from physical (adenoids, tonsil, prostate, tumor), psychological (obsessions, dark thoughts, obsessions, resentment), or emotional blockages (fears, loss of self-confidence, unhappiness).

And then: **either we are lucky enough to still be connected to life intelligence, that will guide us to a therapist. He will help us in our body liberation to quickly recover our health and well-being.**

Or we will be under control of low frequencies to which our deficient and poisoned cells will automatically connect. And we will try to remove these painful and troublesome symptoms as fast as we can. Exactly as if we were turning off the red light in our car, without trying to understand why it lit up.

It will then, stop the liberation process that was supposed to remove the residues, and help us recover a healthy state.

They will remain in our underground layers, and the illusion if being cured will mislead us.

Healed?

Certainly not! Since the poison has not been expelled. It continues to feed our cells which, being more and more affected, function upside down.

Reverse to common sense. They will start to love and ask for the substance that produces the poison in which they are immersed. Under this food addiction, we will more and more love this substance and will consume it eagerly.

And the more we consume it, the more it poisons us!

And this is not all! Concurrently as we forbid our body to evacuate its residues, our immune system forced to silence, will be mute. And of course, we will be connected to lower and lower destroying frequencies.

It is therefore crucial to understand how our body works, not to outreach these limits.

Let us remember that when we come to life, in order to travel our journey, we receive a vehicle, our body, that we will abandon at the end.

Does this vehicle possess a strong constitution and powerful self-defense system?

Due to this rare privilege, we have all the chances to suffer from these violent, even wild, elimination crises, that we call sickness.

Crises, such as those from which our ancestors suffered, through plague and cholera.

The role of these illnesses was to liberate them from starch or charcuterie residues that fed them.

Plague and cholera used our natural elimination ways. Under the influence of fear and ignoring the laws of life, rather than put these sick people to rest on a diet, like animals do when they are wounded or sick, we gathered them and fed them, pretending to support them.

But since the digestive process requires for itself, half of our energy, it is easy to understand that the energy used to digest was not available to eliminate.

These people had all the chances to, sooner or later, be self-poisoned, leading to macabre consequences.

Exactly like it happened in this legendary story: they were not far from recovering health and wellness.

The story took place in Toulouse in the year 1630, during a plague epidemic, when four thieves robbed the dead corpses, without catching the illness. Arrested and condemned to death, they were promised to be saved it they disclosed their secret. It was very simple: it consisted in rubbing one's body with a vinegar in which sage, rosemary, thyme, and lavender had macerated. These plants, like the soap we are using today, are strong anti-bacterial products. The thieves were protected from microbe invasion.

This vinegar, known as "*vinegar of the four thieves*", remained in the French pharmacopeia Codex until 1884.

If we trust this story, old pandemics could have been much less deadly, **if, instead of feeding the "sick" ones to supposedly alleviate them, we had let them fast like wild animals do.**

Just like our dog naturally did, one day, after he had eaten an entire cheese board that I had forgotten in the patio ("*we still ate cheese at that time*"). He woke up the day after, his eyes all yellow, so tired that he remained the whole day in a corner of the kitchen, even refusing the water that I gave him.

After 10 days when he did not move or eat or drink, my husband, seeing him so bad, told me that we should put him down. To which I answered that if our dog were to die, he would do so by himself. 4 days later, that is after 14 days without moving drinking or eating, our dear pet stood up and ran towards the brook where he drank an incredible amount of water. The white of his eyes had turned back whiter, and a week later he was even nicer and vigorous than before his jaundice.

A great opportunity for us to consider the animal's instinctive intelligence!

A kind of intelligence that we, who are supposed to be the cleverest creatures on this planet, seem to have lost. My practice and observation always confirmed that fast and rest, that were the main keys of the ancient doctors, are the first things to do in case of an illness, whatever it is.

This does not mean that these are the only things to do, but they remain the most important...

Let us remember that the women and men of that time, even with their difficult lives, had a mentality, an attitude, a courage and consciousness that we are far from having.

It means that if we had respected our body's fundamental functions, we would not only be healthy, happy, and creative like all mammals on this planet, but could also live

Five times the growing period of our long bones, that is, more exactly, 5 times 20 or 25 years.

Like Jeanne Calment, whose strong constitution allowed her to live 120 years, even though she had a quite common diet.

And what about my fellow colleague Dr Colucci, who started to change his diet after his two brothers got cancer and died very young. He surprised all those who approached him up to the venerable age of 103 years, working with lucidity, and that of 108 years when he left us.

Let us remember that whatever powerful and violent they may be, these elimination crises have no other aim than liberate the body from its residues.

We will qualify them as functional, like the constitutions who are able to endure them.

What have we done with these crises?

In the main situations, still influenced by fear and ignorance of the inverted laws of life to which our poisoned and deficient cells were connected, we "cured" them. Which means that we prevented them from achieving their liberating mission.

And since there was no more elimination or fatigue, fever, discomfort, neither pain, we believed that we were healed.

We did not think of what would occur with these residues, pushed back in the liquids from where they had been extracted, and where, of course, they would not remain silent.

Until the day when a surplus of energy, maybe due to some very energetic food, or to Spring sun, hays, pollens, buds or emotions...Or caused by a shock forcing our body to get rid of everything that overloads it, in search for the perfect balance, it would use this extra energy to try another detox episode.

This time not through our congested and exhausted intestine or kidneys, but with the most resistant rescue system that we have.

Exactly like an aging father would ask his strongest boy to do the tasks that he cannot execute anymore.

Is this system the skin?

In the best case, to compensate for the kidney or urinary work, the skin will evacuate its toxins with substantial sweating, tingling itching, or rash like smallpox, or like it did in pandemics times, with suppurating burning and painful cysts.

Does this rescue system use the respiratory tract?

Still in the best case and to replace the intestines that are now overloaded and lazy, our body will start coughing, sneezing, expectorating these viscosities, as strongly as its energy is important.

Does it lack energy?

Our crisis will be less violent but deeper, like bronchial pneumonia, respiratory congestions, pleurisy. Which are meant to expel the colloidal residues. Or we will get typhoid or puerperal fever, and syphilis. To eliminate our acidic residues.

These crises using a rescue elimination system that still allows our body to get rid of its residues, we also qualify it as *"functional"*.

Not a first-level functional system, like the ones that our kidneys or intestines use, but a second-level one. These crises only weakening the people's and their offspring's constitution, they will be of lower quality and provoke less intense but more profound crises, like tuberculosis, poliomyelitis, called ***"lesional diseases".*** The acidic residues dig caves into our lungs, in which the decomposing colloidal residues will feed a certain virus that Dr Koch discovered. That was tuberculosis. Once again, instead of searching for the cause of this illness, we chose to create a vaccine, preventing our body to free itself from its poisoned overloads. We put these people in sanatoriums where pure air, the only real remedy, overfeeding, and all sorts of surgeries and compressions pretending to cure them, finally forever disable them. This was also the time of unexplained languor, or the starting point of some psychiatric instabilities qualified as imaginary and certainly provoked, as you understand it, by colloidal residues stuck in the brain.

This epoch was also the one of all the "itis" illnesses, like meningitis, encephalitis

Caused by the ejection of our acidic loads through the best and most adapted system, giving them a name ending with "itis". **Not forgetting poliomyelitis, which did so much damage.**

When its only purpose was to liberate the child from the acidic and colloidal residues that he had before he was born, inherited from his lineage.

Like this woman who, when she arrived at my office, instantly told me that she had had poliomyelitis. Seeing my surprised look as she did not show any after effect, she told me that in her village, right after the vaccination, eight out twenty-three children, including the doctor's son, developed a poliomyelitis. Hopefully, her grandmother was a follower of Dr Bartholet's methods, a Swiss doctor in the 1930's, who bequeathed us his wonderful book "La santé par le jeûne" (ndt: "*Healing by fasting*"). Following his advice, she purified the child smoothly, letting her on a diet of diuretic herbal teas and water. Having no other solution, she got her to sweat with hot water bottles. That is all she did, but after one week, all the child's energy having been used to expel the poisoned overload through her feces, urine, and perspiration, **she got up with no trace of any stiffness or deformation.**

While, with all the best intentions, the village's doctor, who had only learnt to neutralize the virus supposed to provoke this terrible illness, set his own son and all his friends in the deforming stage of the illness, making each one of them a life-long cripple.

Is not a good reason to meditate on the wonderful and simple means that nature provides us.

In a nutshell, let's say that the functional crises of great pandemics, the lesional illnesses and crises, with more toxemia and less vitality, led us to weaker but more frequent elimination crises, or to chronic affections, like asthma, eczema, pain, depression, insomnia and allergies.

They have become so frequent that we now call them "diseases of civilization".

These affections, always "cured" without considering what caused them, held back a more abundant and pernicious toxemia, always deeper inside. And slowly but surely, they prepared us to suffer from degenerative illnesses that blossom around us at all ages and in all social environment. Because when the liquids of our body are saturated, they cannot contain any more residues and their only alternative is to get into our cells:

Where they deprogram our brain and create a cancer, all the cancers of this planet.

They paralyze it, they paralyze everything

They sclerose it, create diabetes and sclerosis.

By disconnecting it, they have developed all the murderous and suicidal insanities that flourish more and more these days.

Every month we hear on the radio and TV that a 13- or 14-years old kid killed another one or took his own life.

50 years ago, this would have been unthinkable! It does not mean that today's kids are worse than those of my childhood. No! They are just better "cured" and "fed", the way we do it now.

Which is of course, not my opinion!

It simply means that beside being vaccinated and treated by medicines as they are, no more breast fed but receiving cow milk that was meant for calves, their diet is anarchic. There cells grow more and more poisoned and deficient and connect to the lowest and destructive frequencies that they are able to reach and so, become even more excited and poisoned.

This is of a relentless logic!

This is why every day in France, 400 persons die of a cardio-vascular disease. And according to a famous cancer specialist, one out of three persons currently suffers from cancer. And this is without counting all the hormonal and sexual imbalances, obesity, diabetes, insanity, murder, suicide, of which we never heard as much.

Is this what we expected from progress?

And I am not talking about the genetic impairments that we are preparing for our descendance by eating, drinking, and treating ourselves as we do.

And what about viruses and microbes, will you say?

Nature being our first model, you have probably noticed that flies, bees, and ants flock at speed when you leave some food around.

Just like worms gather from who knows where to devour the corpse of a decomposing animal.

I wonder by what sort of telephone they have been informed, and why would it be different for microbes, flies, or any parasite who have no reason to escape from this rule which says that all what is alive on earth is attracted by its food.

So, I wonder why, same as worms, would not microbes, viruses and all the predators, be necessary for the ecology of our system.

It means that when our body prepares an eliminations crisis, like a good housekeeper, it pulls the furniture aside, empty the drawers, and cleans the corners, to flush out all the dirtiness hidden inside.

It must start by expelling all the toxins out of their enclave and reshape them as they were, before throwing them back into the circulation in charge of taking them to the most appropriate elimination spot.

This transformation revealing a certain state of decomposition and stench, it seems normal that it attracts microbes, viruses, bacillus, and parasites of all kind, who enjoy their favorite food.

This would explain why, when our researchers first saw them multiply under the lens of their brand-new microscope, they genuinely believed that they were the cause of our illnesses.

Exactly as they might have said that it was the worms who killed the corpse that they were eating, or it would be the flies who filled and messed-up the garbage can.

Something no-one would have believed of course.

But under the bright aura of science and progress issued from the low frequencies, we have been taught that it is the microbes who "give" us the illness, and that it was enough to kill them to recover.

Before he left us, the French researcher Louis Pasteur himself is said to have mentioned to one of his collaborators who had always supported this theory:

"*You are right Antoine, microbe is nothing, ground is everything*".

What version of this inverted world did we remember?

The one that asked us to mend our errors or the one that accused the microbes, clearing us from any responsibility? A position that satisfied us, even if such a hypothesis stifled the Hippocratic medicine and favored a symptomatic and artificial point of view that would only combat or suppress our elimination crises, never ever wondering where they came from.

This infernal and subtle scam got us to leave a medicine that respected the laws of life, with its amazing laboratory of senses and perceptions, for a medicine that depends on sophisticated and costly tools all dedicated to analyze the consequences of our inconsistency.

Consequences that wear names, expert names that only its hermetic language could decode. It then dethroned the royal path of commonsense which only wants our good health and well-being and chose the path of nonsense, pretending to heal us but which in fact only gets us ever sicker.

Fortunately, the light over these things starts to light up.

And we can rejoice and try our best to stop criticizing the actions of the inverted world and rather understand how to avoid them.

Some books may enlighten you in this sense:

- "La mafia médicale" ("*The medical mafia*") that Dr Guylaine Lanctôt had the courage to write, and that will explain your things far beyond what you would have imagined.
- "La santé confisquée" ("*The confiscated health*") by Dr Mirko Beljanski. A researcher at the Pasteur Institute, who found a way to protect the healthy cells subject to heavy therapies. He consequently was not promoted as one would think he should have but was dismissed. He was told that the financial report of an AIDS patient was not to be discussed.
- "Sois malade et tais-toi" ("*Be sick and shut up*") by J.J. Rocca, the Director of "Medecines Nouvelles", who will tell you the hidden face of drugs.
- "Cent ans de vaccination et SIDA" ("*One hundred years of vaccinations and AIDS*") by Dr Brouwer
- "Le Rapport Campbell" or in English "*The China study*" by T. Colin Campbell and Thomas M. Campbell. You

will learn the scientific aspect of all what I am telling you naturally.

- "Le sucre, cet ami qui vous veut du mal" ("*Sugar, this evil friend*") by William Dufty. This book is a monument of good sense and truth.

And so many other books that will not, it is true, allow you to recover a healthy state as well as these doctors do:

Bertholet, Salmanoff, Solomidès, Delbet, Kousmine, Joyeux, Lagarde, Vivini...
or all the other doctors or non-doctors, who will show you how far we are from the wonderful Traditional Chinese Medicine, whose ideas built the golden age of China. Whereas, by practicing a medicine that is supposed to be on top of the progress, our world has never been sicker. The role of a genuine medicine should not only be to cure the sick, but to teach us how to be healthy.

Dream, utopia? Certainly not!

Provided that we dethrone the illusions, which made us believe in the sad fatality of catching an illness and in the drugs supposed to heal it. I can imagine you shiver with indignation and call me names, hearing this daring affirmation. Let me tell you that it is not because the prodigious discoveries of science made us dream, that it gave us all what was promised.

Far from it, and the only purpose of this book is to enlighten you, so that you too can rediscover the good sense.

Illnesses

These considerations do not mean that we should live like in Prehistorical or Middle Ages. Not at all! Just like you I appreciate the many improvements of progress. Still, let us not forget that.

The only goal of science is to serve life, not to destroy it!

It is all there, and since we recognize the tree by its fruit, if the fruit is uneatable, let's not blame the fruit but the tree.

Do we have to remind that in the clear blue sky of this new medical practice, soared a little cloud.

Who?

Yes! who can afford to buy these new medications that chemical labs create?

Yes! who can afford to buy these surgeries that make us believe it is a cure-all.

Yes! who can afford that?

Not with a hen or a dozen eggs, like in the old days of medicine, when doctors did not save their knowledge, their effort, but with hard cash.

This is when a new "idea" came...

An idea that suggested to create a new system in which the sick and the healthy would jointly participate, paying a subscription that would raise or diminish, according to the needs of the cause.

The idea seemed meaningful and was immediately accepted.

Although the participation never decreased. And that was done. Under the aura of both progress and science, backed up by the young pharmaceutical industry, the university released a new kind of doctors who, like Dr Knock, suggested that patients visit them regularly.

The social insurance system was of a great help indeed. It fostered the consumption of all these new drugs and surgeries. And as if suddenly all the plants had become poisonous, herbalists' shops were prohibited, forcing the patients, to abandon the use of natural herbs, because they were an awful danger and a rival to the new medications.

A new kind a medicine was born!

Following its advice, we started to consume more and more meat, for its proteins, yoghurts, dairy products and cheese for the calcium, bread, pasta, pizzas, cookies and pastries for their carbohydrates. It led us to more and more often visit the doctors, buy at the drugstore, go to the hospital and also to the unemployment agency or even to court.

Without of course, ever looking back at the real source of our sufferings and illnesses, which are, let us not forget it, only calls for help sent by our body, always in search for its perfect balance.

We have lost a great deal of our instinct and cosmic guidance because of our deficient and intoxicated condition, and the millennium during which we have been consuming cooked food and meat. This treasure that wild animals, who only eat what is planned for them, have preserved.

Instead of searching for the original reason of our illness and trouble, and try to change it, we have strived to make it disappear as fast as possible. We never realized that treating our body as nature wants is not just a question to prevent sickness. Since this sicknesses and pains are just a sort of red light, a whistleblower that our body sends us to correct our behavior.

They ask us to stop poisoning our body and help it get rid of the food residues that don't correspond to its needs. It had therefore to store them into our deepest layers, from where one day, it would try to expel them.

All our sufferings and disorders are not due to misfortune or fatality, but to all our mistakes, to the loss of our cosmic guidance, itself being the consequence of our dietary misbehaviors.

Which means that whatever our afflictions or diseases may be, they serve as an SOS sent by life itself, that warns us to go back to "good sense".

The GOOD SENSE is that of all good deed, engendered by the frequencies of life, whose role is to inform and guide all creatures for their best and that of everyone.

This is how wild animals, who are still connected to the universal intelligence, when there is a tsunami or a great danger, know that they must flee, when humans, who think they are the most advance specie, don't move and are drowned.

The GOOD SENSE that all the religions of the world tried to teach to their believers by choosing the soul and the spirit against the body.

But they did not realize that to love and think, we definitely need our body and its cells. It is true to say that they didn't know that our body was made of wonderful cells, who, alone, allow us to love, to think, act and make of our life a paradise in which nature gave us everything we need. On condition that the cells work as nature planned. But our cells could only become poisoned and deficient and work the wrong way, considering how they have functioned since we started cooking food.

They go reverse to GOOD SENSE...

The sense of life and good deed, to make of our life this paradise that we are all longing for.

This paradise that only exists with a genuine total and natural health, respecting the laws of life.

Vaccinations

This paradise, this wonderful well-being that we yearn for…

Under the aura of science and medicine, we thought that we could reach it. Both were supposed to not only let us believe that they could heal our diseases, but also prevent them.

Vaccination was born!
The absolute miracle!

Of course, in those days, like everyone else, I would have had my kids vaccinated against all the diseases and miseries, including poverty and infidelity…

But luckily, my "invisible teachers" were watching and gave me serious lessons that "vaccinated me against vaccination".

The harshest one was with my second child, Jean-Lou, born on September 30th, who left the hospital before he had recovered his birth weight, and was vaccinated on October 30th. Although he was in a perfect shape, he immediately suffered from important respiratory and bowel trouble that took him to different doctors without any betterment. I ignored at that time, that the great vital force of the child, could not accept such an inconsistent act against life, that vaccination is. Like all the strongest children, he used his energy to get rid of the poisoned heritage that he had received before he was born.

The vaccine's mission was to prevent him to do so!

Since his vaccination, his defense system was strong enough to refuse this anti-natural intervention. Like the strongest children he immediately got sick... To eliminate the residues that he had inherited by birth.

Like all children's disease, the one he was suffering from burst out to help him regenerate.

We knew nothing about this at that time and only wanted to help him recover from this illness by taking him to the doctor's, as we had learnt. In other words, by stopping his little body to unload his poisoned burden and force him to hold it deep inside.

Reason why "well cured", as we believed, beginning of December he suffered from a green diarrhea that led us to this famous pediatrician who immediately prescribed rice water and carrots. It didn't prevent him from getting worse and worse until we had to drive him to the hospital emergencies.

That was at the beginning of January, for a respiratory congestion. He was in the service of that same doctor who called us the day after to urge us to come at once if we wanted to see our little one still alive.

***That was very clear!
Our little boy was dying! No, no, no! Everything in me refused it!***

I suggested my husband to go and see a "hands on healer" that I knew, and he accepted to come.

We lived near Belfort that year of 1954. The temperature was minus 63°F (-17°C) and roads were closed to traffic. Despite these conditions, we went to the healer's place and he accepted to accompany us to the hospital. But visits were closed, and we could not come in. Refusing to resign, we went to the pediatrician who was totally unyielding to the idea, when Mr. Hiffnecker, the healer, said something like:

"If the little what-his-name had had... he wouldn't have died..."

I ignore what he was talking about, but I remember that she called her service at the hospital and asked that little Grosjean would be left in the "gallery" for ten minutes. Jean-Lou was under oxygen since the day before and when the nurse took him out of his oxygen chamber, he was so pale that without his sigh we could have believed he was dead. The gallery was under a patio outside the hospital whose windows were frosted, and where it was as cold as outside. This temperature difference could have been fatal to him, but we had not even thought of it. After having laid him on a table, Mr. Hiffnecker put his hands over, gently and continuously, from the head to the toes of the child, just a few centimeters from his body, which he was turning, on the back and the front.

How long did it last? I do not know.

But after a moment, each time his hands were above the child's chest, his sighs disappeared, and when his hands left, they started again. A few minutes after, I saw some little tiny red sticks that seemed to adjust on his face. I was astounded by these little capillaries that started to blush his face. At the same time his little hands started to move, and his lips opened.

Our little boy seemed to go back to life.

Time, cold, did not exist anymore.

Our heart was beating so fast, and as if to take us back to reality, the nurse took back the child and brought him back to his oxygen chamber. The healer proposed to come back the day after, and maybe another day, to secure his work. He also said that his parents' faith was not stranger to the baby's recovery.

And this was with our heart full of gratitude and hope that we drove him back home.

The following day arriving at the hospital, we were prevented to come in. Whatever! Like we had done the previous day, we went to the doctor's and waited until she took her last patient to the door. Pretending not to see us, she let them out through the entrance door. Despite the temperature of -17°c my husband and Mr. Hiffnecker waited outside, while I came into the waiting room where she only condescended to look at me when all her patients had gone, saying as an excuse:

Misses Grosjean, yesterday you were like a mother gone mad, you might have reached for the stars to save your child. But today this is over. This morning, the entire hospital mocked me, so I think you will understand that this is not acceptable, this is over. If you want your son to be treated by a healer, then you will have to take him out of the hospital.

No, doctor! I do not want less but more for my son! And as she showed unshakable, I heard myself say: "*If the baby recovers everything will be alright, but if he doesn't, between, God, you and me, one will know who is responsible, won't we?*"

And without being able to do anything more for our baby, we went back home, where I stayed the whole time, he remained the at the hospital, connected with my mind. Even at night when I feared he could be in danger if I fell asleep. I spent my time imagining him, talking to him, see him grow up and become an adult, a father, a grandfather. Two weeks passed, too long weeks until the doctor called us to tell that our boy was out of danger, and that in such cases one had to stay two or three more months at the hospital. But she added that in our case, it was not necessary.

No need to say that after this experience, none of our children and grandchildren ever got vaccinated.

This has not prevented them from studying and for some of them, to travel the world, thanks to I must say, the precious recommendations of a Professor in the faculty of medicine, Dr Jean de Goldfiem, whom I was lucky to meet in a conference, where he mentioned that if we didn't want to vaccinate our children, which he totally understood, we just had to write to the school doctor in these terms: ***"Doctor, I totally agree that my child be vaccinated. Under condition, though, that you write me a certificate guarantying that you take all responsibilities in case of primary and secondary side effects that may occur following the vaccination. Respectfully yours etc."***

Wasn't that excellent? Such attitude forces those who impose them, to totally honor their convictions. Which didn't prevent me for asking myself whether it had been the vaccine that was dangerous, or if, in this very case, it might have set off as a triggering element of the child's vitality to help him get rid of his heavy colloidal inheritance.

This was not exempt of risk in our ignorance of that time, and would become less risky, knowing what I know now. Exactly as it happened for this strong girl in the swiss mountains, whom I mentioned above. Would this mean that the great vital force of children did not accept the vaccine, which is meant to prevent them from eliminating their poisoned heritage? But on the contrary, it had given them an opportunity to eliminate?

~ ***I am really tempted to believe so!*** ~

Whereas in a number of cases, when the vaccine works, which means prevents them from eliminating their poisoned heritage, their little body will have to retain it deeper in the hidden layer, always more intensely poisoning the environment in which its cells bathe. This will lead the whole immune system to weaken.

Reason why our world, fed and cured the way it is, works more and more reverse to good sense.

How could we elude this more and more common illness once considered as the millers' disease?

I am talking about asthma, which is extremely frequent is Asia, where the common diet is made of rice which, refined as our bread and pasta are, is an important source of colloidal intoxication. Asthma tells us its intimate relation with phlegm and viscosities that are produced, we know it, by an incomplete digestion of carbohydrates.

Asthma was extremely rare in times when vaccines did not exist and could therefore, expectorate a great part of their colloidal heritage through terrible but liberating pertussis.

This means that by vaccinating our children against pertussis, we have prevented them to eliminate through coughing and spewing, the abominable mucus that they had inherited, and forced them to hold it profoundly into the depth of their underlayers, where they upholstered the inside of their respiratory alveolus. Then their breathing capacities being reduced, their blood lacked in oxygen.

This induces a cardiac fatigue that expresses with bluish lips and extremities when the weather cools down or when the sick person endures some difficulties. At least until he becomes stronger to expel all the reduced and dried viscosities stuck deep inside his alveolus where they are kept, upholstering them. **Their swelling, in order to be expectorated, thus created that kind of suffocation provoking the asthma crises.**

This suffocation disappears as soon as the sick person can at last spit out, or even better, expel all his phlegm and viscosities in a sticky diarrhea for the best. All this only means that the body finally finds its natural way to eliminate, which are the intestines.

You perhaps find my deductions rather simple or even simplistic?

This is your right. But I learnt from experience that we should better replace bread, potatoes, and rice that asthmatics love by fruits and sprouted seeds, to stop being asthmatic, rather than try to stop the crises with medicines. Those, by exciting their cardiac system, lead them to exhaustion. This is why asthmatic people do not die because of asthma itself, but of heart failure, like my husband when he was 44 years old.

How not to speak about the flu vaccine that the elderly commonly receives? This flu that, at least once a year, allows them to get rid of their poisoned loads, through urine, feces, and perspiration, without forgetting the cough and sputum. Could this explain why our seniors who are perfectly vaccinated, do not get flu anymore, but instead are more and more affected by Alzheimer.

But who will link these two diseases, apparently so different?
Statistics? Not at all!
They are much more rewarded to speak out that thanks to vaccines, the average lifespan has raised. Without explaining what "living" means.

Because if this happened to my father who died at the age of 82, I must admit that in the conditions how he lived, he did well to leave us the way he did.

Although he had been vaccinated against flu for twenty years, he suffered from quite a strong one, that led him straight to the hospital, from where I admit, he went out a few days after, totally cured.

Still, this little precision needs to be disclosed. If he had entered the hospital in a normal intellectual and psychological shape, when he came back, he could not utter a word.

Surprising?
No, it is the contrary that should

Because through healing, that is by stopping this elimination crisis called flu, his phlegm and residues trying to escape, finally invaded his cerebral liquids, making them thicker and viscous. This prevented the brain connections to work normally.

Just like it happened to old persons who were said to fall back into childhood. Not because of vaccines which did not exist yet, but because by invading the cerebral liquids, the lifelong accumulated toxemia prevented their cells to connect normally.

What I am trying to say, if I can insist on that point, is that if I don't totally agree with vaccination, I am tempted to say that it might not be the real cause, but still and always, the triggering factor on our food residues. And if there are no residues, there is no reason to get sick.

Constitutions

This means that it should be enough to eat healthily and treat our body correctly like nature wants, to be in a perfect shape, and stay connected to the universal life intelligence, in charge of informing us all life long, to help us create a happy and accomplished life.

This is perfectly true!

"Look for the realm of Heaven and the rest will be added on to you", said our old priest in his Sunday preaches. It made the little girl whom I was, dream, spending the greatest part of her life searching for this heavenly kingdom and perhaps find it, because what else could it be but health?

Health, that we care for once we seem to lose it. This health without which we make of our young people, unemployed, rebellious, excluded, drug addicts, suicidal kids, or gangsters. Whereas with health we are alive, courageous, creative, and happy.

Health, the only thing that keeps us Living Really Alive!

This does not mean that we should never be sick! Because sickness is in fact just a way to protect and improve our health! When I talk about sickness, I mean of course these eliminations functional and lesional crises, which, after being "cured" as we were taught, have created the real, degenerative illnesses.

Some swiss insurance companies even propose to pay for the health education of their clients. These enterprises are *not* nonprofit, so if they do so, it is because they found an interest in it.

Especially if we consider that the expense for one month of natural treatment, including some dietary supplements, that are indeed costly, corresponds to a single hospital day. And the result is even better. One should know that once a person has learnt how to recover her health, she has also understood how to preserve it, as well as the joy of living, the happiness, and creativity that come with it.

Can someone challenge this profitability?

Moreover, a healthy person is a blessing for herself and the community, whereas a sick or unhappy person is a financial burden, a source of expenses for herself and for everyone. And this is without considering all the pain that she imposes, against her will, to her relatives.

When will there be a bonus for health and a malus for sickness?
Yes! When?

It will happen when the majority of us will have understood that suffering and illness are not a fatality, but rather a red light lit in our heart, head or body, by the life intelligence, to warn us that there is something to modify in our behavior.

But since by feeding and curing ourselves the way we do, we have swapped our cosmic universal guidance to that of the inverted intelligence, it is very difficult for us to understand this.

Our guidance that connects us to the real wealth of life, whose role seems to be the same as that of our body's cells. **In other words, work by and for one another, to serve the whole while serving ourselves.**

Whereas, blinded by the dazzling aura of illusion and fake wealth, the inverted intelligence got us dependent, unhappy, sick, and moronic consumers, whatever it looks like.

The first ones are always happy to live, and the second are not.

This is the reason why we must understand that if we are where we are now, it is, before all, because we replaced our access to the real wealth of life with illusory benefits, only driven by profit.

Even though it brings suffering, illness, or war... I am not criticizing anyone, do believe me, this is simply a statement.

If we created social welfare to be forgiven, we forgot that the true role of society is not to give a fish to the hungry one, but to teach him how to catch it. As well as we are not supposed to fight against dishonesty and crime, but rather to encourage and develop the potential qualities of each one. **And please let me repeat that fighting and struggling are and only are behaviors that lead to more victims.**

For this reason, instead of fighting against your pains and diseases, I encourage you to learn how to take care, develop and sometimes recover your most precious asset: your health! Which is not the easiest of things, it is true. It will require a certain determination as well as some knowledge about how your constitution works.

If we have a body made with a head, two arms and legs, it is also true that each one of us is unique. So, it is advisable that, to treat ourselves better, we remember this well.

Did not the old Socrates tell us:

> ***"To know thyself is the beginning of wisdom"***

As it is a fact that we can burn green wood in a high draught chimney without being smoked out, it is also true that a low draught chimney needs dry wood and frequent sweeping. Exactly like a first level constitution. We can afford some food extras sometimes when others with a weaker constitution cannot accept them.

Do we have the privilege to have a first level constitution?

In this more and more scarce situation, our body is strong and harmonious. The features of our face are perfectly shaped, and our eyes nicely open, reveal a strong neuro-glandular system.

Are our nostrils largely open? They reveal a strong respiratory system, and nice plump lips say that we have a good digestive system. Especially if they open on strong teeth.

We also have a solid bone structure, a strong musculature, a high vitality and generally an excellent immune system. Being naturally sober, our complexion is clear like people who have a good elimination system. And as we sleep well, we do not need much to feel fit and in a good mood.

It means that with such a constitution, not only are we still connected to the frequencies of life, the ones that make us naturally cheerful, happy, and creative, but also do we benefit from an exceptional health and an unforeseen resistance.

But and this is not as positive, if we have such a constitution, we also have the best chances to suffer from violent elimination crises. But and this is more reassuring, if we are able to help our body achieve these crises, it will be easier and faster to heal.

Do we have a weaker, called second level, constitution?

Still rather young, our body started to lose its beauty, its resistance and density, and also had tendency to wrap, swell or slim easily.

With a less sharp design than in the previous constitution, our features show a too loose or tight texture of our skin. With a narrow opening, our nostrils reveal a shrunk respiratory system and if our eyes are not as wide, the neuro-glandular system may be weakened. Then, if too thick, our lips mean a hepatic overload, whereas if they are lean or not showing at all, it is rather an acidic surcharge due to a renal or urinary deficiency.
All signs of a sort of degeneration from which the heirs of these constitutions have more or less inherited. One of course, does not need to have all these signs all together, to belong by one or the other constitution.

This constitution being the most frequent by these days, you might, just like me, belong to it.

In this case, and as long as you have not done what is necessary to clean and regenerate it, you will continue to prefer the food or stimulants that have poisoned you the most.

This will increase your difficulties to assimilate, eliminate and will engender other problems like weight gain or loss, or maybe insomnia or constipation, hyper or hypo blood pressure, cholesterol overload, migraines. All these difficulties will compromise your mental balance, your psyche and body. Your elimination crises will then be much less violent but more frequent, nay chronic, and more difficult to manage than in the first level constitution.

Has the quality of our constitution continued to damage?

The ones belonging to this third level constitution will be even more deficient and intoxicated and will also have a weaker immune system than in the previous constitutions. Their affections will no more be functional or lesional, but chronic, like diabetes, obesity, asthma, insomnia, anxiety, dark thoughts, depression... Trying to alert them that they suffer from colloidal clog, whereas type 1 diabetes, eczema, pain, back ache, migraines, hemorrhoids, painful menstruations, violence, anger... inform them of an acidic or crystalloid burden. And let us not forget the psychological and mental disorders that come with it and have created all the ailing ones that this planet bears, and to which this constitution gave birth.

Once again, do we understand these symptoms and are we willing to learn how to treat them the way they should rebuild our good health?
Or shall we continue to take pills and drugs that hide the sufferings and misdeeds created by our drifts?

Then we will continue to fall deeper and have all these degenerative illnesses like heart failure, cancer, multiple sclerosis, Parkinson disease, suicidal or murder tendencies... And of course, all the unhappy people of the earth, physically, psychologically, and emotionally.

Were we conceived by our parents under this fourth level constitution?

Which, just like the previous one, is not the result of chance or fate, but of a collective ignorance and unconsciousness which, through our mistakes, has succeeded in deteriorating, damaging, sclerosing our genes and thus making all the genetic diseases that are constantly developing.

This is why we will conclude by saying that persons with a functional constitution are like a hot fireplace. That is to say that they can eat anything they want, and still stay in a good shape. For a moment only, because behaving that way, they put themselves at risk and might age in a worse shape, and also pass a weaker constitution to their offspring.

As the common saying goes: *"when parents drink, children toast".*
Let us say that people with a functional constitution have almost disappeared and those with a lesional constitution should eat the most energetic possible nutrients, that leave little residues. It is necessary and even essential that they experience some detox crises in order to regain their natural health and balance.

For the degenerative constitution people, if they are not sick yet, they should know that it is in their interest to follow the rules of life if they want to avoid illness.

And if they already are, they should know that health restoration is possible. But it will require more time and knowledge, and sometime the addition of multiple types of techniques and medicines to reach a happy conclusion.

They also should be aware that their chances will decrease as they progressively receive chemical treatments and surgeries. Because even though these treatments have a punctual positive outcome, they cannot have an effect without weakening their immune system.

A great idea would be to integrate them the best possible way, by a new manner of practicing medicine.

For the genetic constitution, even if their interest is to live as naturally as possible, they shouldn't expect any spectacular regeneration, because all what was destroyed before birth and considering our current knowledge, has little chance to be rebuilt.

Anyway, as long as there is life, there is hope, and a miracle is always possible.

The most important is to do our best not to get to this scenario.

This takes us to the reason why we should know what to expect from our constitution for the great, unique, and valuable interest of learning how to treat it as it should. And for the simple reason that

Prevent is better than cure.

Glues and viscosities

We lost the paradise given by nature because we keep on living, feeding, and treating ourselves as we did since we started cooking food, in good conscience, or more accurately, in complete unconsciousness. We made of our lives an infernal succession of sufferings, shortages, conflicts, wars, and illnesses.

It also means that if we are able to go back to the starting point and modify our lives, we will automatically meet the "*good sense*" of life with again all its beneficence.

The good sense!

We all would like to live healthy and in happiness.
The good sense will allow us to improve, develop or find health, by respecting the basic laws of our functioning. Remember the first ones: breathing and feeding, from which the quality of our sleep and the elimination processes depend. However, before we address these issues in a practical and constructive

manner, let me tell you the consequences that this wrong way to treat and feed ourselves had on our physical, psychological, and mental health.

Let us start, if you will, with these not painful, but annoying troubles and sicknesses caused by the residues of slow sugar that we consume instead of the fast-acting sugar coming from the trees of our good old planet earth.

These residues are, as you know it now, the phlegm and viscosities that our body couldn't drain into our feces, and which, according to our constitution and other considerations, had the opportunity to dwell in our adenoids and tonsils, causing them to swell.

We cut them off, without modifying what altered them. Exactly like a plumber who cuts off a syphon when it is clogged instead of cleaning it and putting a grid at one end, so that it does not block again. A fast and efficient technique for sure, at first sight at least.

And we can guess that the next time we call the plumber, he will have to go deeper inside to search for the waste that the missing syphon has not retained. The same way, we will have to reach the most unexpected places to remove the mucus and phlegm of our tonsils or adenoids.

In the thyroid for example, where reduced and lyophilized, they remain and slow down the functions.

Leading to hypothyroidism and its regrettable consequences like obesity, among others.

Or maybe they will turn into a small dump that we call nodule or tumor. This will not only require a surgery but will also forever change the life without ever asking why **what needs to be removed with a scalpel, did not need one to appear.**

Do they set up in our sinuses?

They will turn into small crystals, waiting for a surplus of energy, to escape with a strong sinusitis.

Or they might also, in case of a weaker immune system, build **this embarrassing goiter,** whose bearer in my childhood, all suffered from all kinds of respiratory problems.

Did I tell you that mucus is at the origin of all the disturbing, uncomfortable and painless troubles of humanity?

Aren't they also the ones that drop from the female genital organs, turning into slimy losses commonly known as vaginal discharge and that I use to name "vaginal flu"?

This discharge, white in the best conditions, will turn into colored, brownish, green, and smelly material as the toxemia increases. Constantly pushed back each time it tries to go out of the body, it will finally decompose and turn into a smelly infection with following problems. Like the invasion of our reproduction organs, leading to **frigidity, impotence, and sterility.**

Mr. Martin de Beauce, an early French naturopathic practitioner, explained with his good sense, that **a constipated woman who also had blood flow disturbances, had all the chanced to grow a uterine fibroma.**

I always noticed that when the decomposition of feces in the lower intestine is next to the blood of menstruations, this putrid surrounding necessarily favors such development. It proves us, once again, that a uterine fibroma can only develop with the food they eat.

These viscosities again, that covered the baby's heads of my childhood when they were strong enough to produce seeping and sticky cradle caps. And now lacking energy, today's children have replaced them with eczema and later at adolescence, by acne. it can also manifest as multiple warts, small tumors, or frequent lipomas.

We find them again inside our lungs' alveoli, where, like sails in the wind, they provoke this noisy snoring, so annoying for the partner. A medical congress in Montpellier called them "snoropathies" and the only medical answer was surgery.

Them again who, by enveloping our vocal cords, have veiled, broken or extinguished our voice? Or once on our cornea, they prepare the future cataract of our old days and in our thickened blood, called sometimes "hemogliasis".

And them again that paralyze the irrigation of our eyes, leading us to weaken or lose sight.
When mixed with the crystalloid residues in our ears and trying to escape from our ear canal, they gently but surely prepare **the deafness of our old days.** When too abundant in our blood vessels, they dilate and expand them, creating **graceless varicose veins and painful hemorrhoids**. This mucus again, that slow down the blood circulation and cause us heavy legs, and when they mix

up with the crystalloid residues, cause even **high blood pressure and other consequential disorders**. Always them, when clogging the interior of our blood vessels, they create a **coronary insufficiency, an arteritis,** or "curdling" our blood they make **thrombosis** that might paralyze us or even **shorten** our earthly journey.

Here they are again, invading our liver, they urge it to relieve itself through liver inflammations causing **hepatitis, called A, B, C or D?**

All this, according to the existence, the nature and abundance of our residues, that a prodigious vaccine will try to lock down. When, whatever hepatitis it may be, its role is to alert us that our liver is packed and tries to expel the mucus and viscosities that invade it.
The "hepatic" constitution incidentally prefers her worse enemies, bread, pasta, and everything made out of flour and starch, to which it will add fat if his gallbladder is congested. **And let us not forget its favorite stimulant food, chocolate, that contains theobromine**, each time its congested liver needs help.

Isn't it the mucus that, slowing down the flow of our gallbladder, provokes constipation? This is a new way for intoxication, which, by raising the volume of our decomposing feces in the large intestine, will enlarge and dilate it under the scholar name **dolichocolon when it stretches out, and megacolon when it enlarges.**

You must confess that it will be easier to tell your friends that you have a dolichocolon or a megacolon, rather than say that your intestines are full of putrid sh...

This quite different way of seeing things will make you, in the first case, feel proud of this anomaly that make you so special, while waiting for a medical miracle, and in the second, not willing to praise what is in your bowels, you will do everything to get rid of **the putrefaction in your intestines, that gives you bad breath**, swells you with gas which expel with smelly winds, revealing an intestinal dirtiness **where grow worms, pests, candida, colibacillosis, and other known predators.** All of them who find in these putrid fermentations, everything they need to multiply.

Them again who, slowing down your saturated pancreas activity, will prevent it from secreting the necessary insulin to transform sugar. One will then suffer from **hyperglycemia**, that will soon turn into **diabetes**, and if ever the patient in a self-destructive attitude, suffers from bulimia, this will drive him to **obesity or comatose state.** These are real distress warnings saying that it is urgent to alleviate the digestive system.

Will this patient hear and do what is necessary to improve the situation?

Or perhaps, not being understood, will he be overmedicated, which, far from providing the illusion of a better state, will turn the viscosities and mucus into master pieces for

all the fear, worrying, nightmares, and dis-ease.

which are in reality the product of a thick, viscous, too sweet blood, that slows down the brain, and that is the starting point of pessimism, negativity, and creates most of **our relational, professional or any sort of failures.**

Will these sticky viscosities be able to block some of our connections? We will have **fixed ideas, or obsessions** that will limit us in our actions. Will they pass into our lymph? They will produce phlegmatic people with **shy attitudes, sadness, and anxiety,** adding their sinister collaboration to **break ups, divorces, or jobs loss.**

This is just a glimpse on the disastrous consequences that these ruthless residues can have on our health. And this is not all, because when they cannot drain out from our body through intestines, lungs, skin, or genital way; they finally use the renal way which is totally unfit for this. Destroying our kidneys which then, will no more be able to eliminate the acidic residues in our pale as water urine, instead of being golden yellow. Our Ancestors used to say:

"golden yellow pee, gold pee".

Acids and crystals

"Golden yellow pee, gold pee".

So, our forbear had observed that when the urines were pale like water, it meant that they did not contain the acids that they should eliminate. These acidic residues that blood brings to the kidneys in charge of filtration and elimination through urine.

Something that our kidneys cannot operate when they are filled with viscosities. In such a case, they drive them back into the arterial circulation, among other effects. **They will oxidize blood, destroy iron which is indispensable to make red blood cells.** We will suffer from anemia at a lesional level or even leukemia at the degenerative level.

Or people might suffer from hemophilia, which was the disease of rich people and nobles, mostly fed with meat, game and alcohol.

Unless, like the acid flowing into pipes until it drills them, this excess of uric acid in the blood vessels finally weakens them to cause **an internal hemorrhage**. Or like a river drops its sand when it slows down, our blood leaves the acids in our joints and **gives us all kinds of joint pains and rheumatisms.**

Unless they prefer to settle in the intervertebral discs where they will herniate the discs, or in the back muscles that will give us that famous back pain that is so common nowadays.

Or on its way, it could leave it in a bag, like the gallbladder. Its reduced flow aimed at saponifying fat from our food, will make cholesterol that deposits along our arteries, clogging them and making arteritis.

Another possibility is that they remain in the form of sands, where they will mix with colloidal residues in a first stage, building **sludge and lithiasis.** And in a second stage, these stones that our body will attempt to eliminate with very painful crises called **renal colic for kidneys, and hepatic colic for the gallbladder.**

Shall we understand this painful phenomenon, and help our body accomplish its salutary work and drive things back to normal? Or shall we just dissolve these lithiasis, remove the gallbladder and the stones, without changing anything to the diet that provoked them. Of course, we will benefit from a short-term remission. Will these tiny crystals finally abrade our nerves? We will suffer from **neuralgia, neuritis, sciatica.** Will they settle in our tendons and cartilage? Then it will be a **tendonitis, tennis-elbow, and all sorts of pains** due to the accumulation of the residues repeatedly laid off in our body by our blood.

They can also destroy and burn our cartilage like it is the case each time we have to replace a meniscus, a patella, or a femoral neck?

To correctly understand the insidious action of these little crystals, let us remember that they do not hurt when solid. They silently abrade the tissues and organs that they touch.

But when the body tries to eliminate them, they have to liquify like snowflakes that melt, and pass in the urine or perspiration in order to be eliminated.
This transformation from solid to liquid state will reveal their acidic nature.
Then will burn our nerves and provoke all the pains we know.

We try to get rid of these pains using analgesics and anti-inflammatories whose only goal is to desensitize our nerves and continue with our dietary errors that, slowly but surely, lead us to a **circulatory accident, arthrosis, osteoporosis, poly arthritis, cancer or any other degenerative illness always painful, invalidating and paralyzing.**

I want to tell you what happened to one of my brothers who, very young, suffered from psychological disorders that cumulated with physical painful problems.

That's why he spent his life going to therapists who tried to relieve him, until one day he found a miraculous remedy that stopped his pain, while he could continue to eat cheese and delis that he was fond of, and to drink as much coffee as he wanted. One year after he retired, while he was picnicking with his wife, just after eating his lunch he stood up, staggered, turned blue and fell down. He was dead.

Surprising?

Not at all, but the contrary should be.

Because painkillers and anti-inflammatory drugs do like cutting the wire of the firemen's telephone when the house is on fire, so that the brain or the fire brigade are not disturbed. This will not prevent the house from burning, neither the acid to deteriorate our blood vessels and one day cause a breach with internal bleeding, followed by death, like for my brother.

Have these little crystals, yes them again, seeped into our bone tissue?

My grandfather was very proud to have kept all his teeth until his late age when he passed away. Even with toothpaste, a brush, and cares like he never had, his grandchildren will not have this privilege.

It is true that he ate meat only once a week, and not every week, and a Camembert would feed three persons for a whole week. It turned so dry that we had to break the last pieces to eat them. Just as we had desserts only on holy days, that were not often. He used to drink a whole barrel of ash tree water made with the leaves of the ash tree, supposed to help eliminate the acids. This is without considering that not only the dentists, but also the oculists and opticians have become richer with these crystals. This, of course, is not a judgment against these professions that we are happy to find when we need them, but rather against us who were not able *not to need* them.

As we did not understand the signs of the uveitis, conjunctivitis, or sties of our childhood, that were saturated by the crystals in our eye liquids. Our sight weakened so that seeing became difficult if not impossible.

Sixty years ago, in a classroom, only three children out of thirty wore spectacles. Nowadays, we could almost say that three out of thirty do not wear them.

Progress? For whom?

I will add that the persons I saw become blind before the age of fifty, ate loads of cheese and dairy products.

These little crystals also tried to escape from our auditory canal, causing the **aching otitis of our youth.**

Could we perceive them with dry and damaged hair? Beside the shampoos and specific lotions that we gave them, we continued to eat meat and cheese and to acidify our blood, that not only blazed the minerals that our hair need to be shiny and strong, but also burned their roots.

Causing their fall that we have described as baldness and called hereditary, without realizing that paternal baldness was already the ransom of those who could afford to eat meat every day.

Did they warn us of their undesirable presence by bitten, stained, brittle or grooved nails, or did they choose skin as a means of escape? If we have a strong vital potential, we will suffer from itching, redness, rash, or all sorts of unbearable burns. With less potential, we have eczema, herpes, psoriasis, shingles, crevasse, and vitiligo. Antalgics or corticoids have tried to make them disappear by stimulating our adrenal glands. Once they are drained, we get a degenerative illness like a giant lupus, or any such illness.

How many “well treated” skin rash turned into cancers?

Maybe you remember that our forebears, who were stronger than us, suffered from painful abscesses expelling their poisoned loads. And maybe some of you will remember these doctors or veterinarians who, some fifty years ago, practiced fixation abscesses for all the chronic illnesses they could not cure.

Knowing that they might have a chance to cure them if the abscess got ripe and ejected the “bad blood”, whereas the prognostic was rather negative for those who could not.

Nowadays we barely have abscesses, but we do have cyst and tumors. I like to call them abscess buds that, because the lack of energy cannot drive their load out of the skin barrier. In general, we could say that hard cysts are of crystalloid origin, and the soft painless ones are of colloidal origin.

Have these tiny acids invaded the deep layers of our skin? It may lose its precious and subtle role of exchanging air, waves, and fluids, as well as its thermo-regulating function, which, even where we are in a 95°F (35°C) temperature, will force us to wear a sweater. And it will also lose its elasticity during pregnancy, causing ugly stretch marks or even a need for surgery.

Will they escape through a wound, even if we do everything to heal it? We will have a varicose wound meant to evacuate the poisons that could not escape through the natural ways. Do we still block it inside the body? It will be almost impossible and may lead to an internal bleeding.

Or maybe our body will transfer this load to some other emunctory which can be genital, cerebral, digestive, ocular, or any other. Will they penetrate the cells' liquids? This will turn into ungraceful cellulite like newborn babies have nowadays.

Will they use the menstruations to escape?

They will hurt as much as the acid load is important. But whatever! Just do a hysterectomy and that is over. No uterus, no pain!

What will the female body do with all these un-expelled residues in the absence of menstruation?

Either they will go into the blood circulation, or like a rope pulling a too heavy load, the heart will do too much effort to drain these toxins into the venous circulation which, much too congested, will cause high blood pressure.

Once again, the best way to recover a lower blood pressure is not to fluidify the blood with drugs, but to clean it from its residues.

What if the crystals, them again, settle in our digestive membranes? We will have acidity and heartburn which are the first signs of ulcer. And according to where exactly they are, we call them stomatitis, gastritis, ulcer, or fistula.

Our body requiring a certain effort to evict them, we will call them, depending on which system they use, spasm, hepatic, intestinal or renal colic. If they lay down in the gallbladder, making it ineffective, it will provide constipation, another source of intoxication. And this is without considering the making of fat that our overburdened body is unable to burn and reduce, and that we store the most graceless way.

Do they maybe prefer to go into the pancreas? Its sclerosed cells being unable to produce insulin, we will suffer from pancreatitis, or perhaps, during adolescence, did it try to warn us with diabetes signs. Or maybe repetitive otitis and strep throats told us that we had an important acidic charge causing migraines, panic disorder, insomnia or excitement states, anger, and violence. Even if they maybe show up in specific emotional conditions, these are still a consequence of the acids.

What if they settle in the thyroid? We will firstly have hyperthyroidism, and then the inevitable depression.

Excitement automatically turns into depression

Have they deteriorated the nerves that close our anal or urinary sphincter? Like an old rubber band, it will not contain our feces or urines any longer and we will have to wear diapers, like babies.

Did they burn and demineralize some organs, causing them to collapse? We will have a stomach, pelvis, kidneys descent, that will be partly solved with surgery, but not really, since it should be with a diet corresponding to our physiological needs.

If not, the digestion will be more and more difficult, because the only choice left for food will be to ferment in our stomach. Who, unable to clear out, will distend, offering a putrid decomposing and smelly matter, to all the worms, parasites, colibacillosis, candida's or other pests enjoying this poisoned magma?

Did they invade our brain and nervous system?

By destroying the minerals that are essential for our cells to reach the high frequencies they will bring us to lower and destructive states of consciousness, feelings, and ideas. This can only favor the ultimate stage of illness, which are cardiovascular diseases, cancers, paralysis, madness, suicides, that our poisoned and de-connected world perfectly creates but so hardly treats.

As we have seen for the glues and viscosities, this succinct picture of the consequences of our crystallized residues in our life and health.

Psychic and mental illnesses

How could we forget to mention Doctor Alexis Carrel's work, who, in the beginning of the 20th century, accomplished the feat of maintaining embryo chicken cells alive for 23 years, as mentioned in some books, or 32 in others.

Maybe a printing error, but still a lifespan that the oldest hens of our barns, never reached. These cells died the only day when the water in which they were kept, had not been changed. Which leaves no doubt about the importance of the liquids' cleanliness in which cells reside.

We all experienced that we are easily in a bad mood if we did not sleep enough or if we drank or ate too much. These elements have consequences on our behavior.

And about the "de-feat of the after feast", rare are the ones who never experienced it, after the euphoria of the feast, partly resulting from wine, alcohol, meat, treats and pasties' overconsumption.

The drug addicts call this a “coming off”, a downturn that asks for more and more drug and provides less and less euphoria, a state of mind that should be ordinary, and that they seek so desperately. This shows the importance of the fuel that we put in our body, even if it behaves differently in each one of us.

We all know that some people get miserable or others happy with wine. Some get terribly angry if they drink too much. We know that the same person can be an angel when sober, or a demon with alcohol. And for those who doubt, **the delirium tremens of alcoholics is a sufficient proof.**

I remember the annual village festival when I was little. Even if they were worried about it, women prepared quantities of meat and sweet desserts. And also, good bottles and moonshine that men drank more than usual on that day.

And at the end of the meal, they told stories, laughed, and sang. Until one of them, for some silly reason, started a dreadful fight ending in tears and cries, provoking a clash that colloidal type's persons would keep for years and maybe generations.

Isn't it at weekends and during holidays that fights, and accidents occur?

They are not only due to tiredness, but also good meals, coffee and of course alcohol whose misdeeds are famous and that new generations are more and more seeking.

And let's talk about industrial sugar, chocolate and cheese, apparently harmless, but whose poisons originate not only all the physical illnesses and all the troubles and sickness that the old generations called imaginary and that we now qualify as psychological and mental.

Psychological when these ideas make you suffer or lose your mind.

Mental when the feelings hurt the heart.

Like physical troubles and illnesses, psychological and mental problems are painful if their origin is crystalloid, and not painful but annoying and tedious if their origin is colloidal. Once again, the most important is not to analyze the patient's symptoms with a scientific name but rather to consider his constitution, vitality, nature, and importance of his toxemia which observation and study are still fundamental for a real recovery.

Like for physical illnesses, the strongest patients will have sharp and functional crises. The weakest will have lesional and chronic crises and the most intoxicated not having enough strength for any crisis, will engender the poor and miserable fellows of all kinds.

These three stages represent the seriousness of the person's health condition, as well as her recovering capacities. The latter follow the same principles as physical disorders which is that, whatever powerful and violent their crises are, the healing of people with a functional constitution will be easier and faster than for the ones with a lesional constitution, whose recovery will be slower and touchier.

The crystalloid or acid crises of the functional constitutions express through violent and harsh angers, whereas for lesional constitutions it will rather be blockages, sulkiness, fixed ideas, grudge, or confinement.
As too much electricity will cause a storm, it is the excess of uric acid in the brain liquids that provokes this incontrollable drive called anger or violence. And the excess of viscosities will rather block the language and create resentment.

Once again, glues and crystals associate with the person's vitality and the capacity of its immune system, will create suffering, psychological and mental misery. This absolute principle will even manifest by mixing both elements, to the point that we cannot distinguish them anymore.

It is generally meat, dairy products and stimulants that make crystals, which, since the beginning of times, built the dominating warriors and gangsters who rule the world.
While soups and cereal mush, starches and veggies have confined the colloidal natures in their shyness, fears, and passivity, turning them into submissive and "kind" people who can be exploited.

I am convinced that if the Germans had not been fed with beer and cold meats during the last world war, they would never have done what they did.

You may say, like I often heard, that Hitler was vegetarian. Firstly, I would like to see a proof of that, and if ever he was, I would like to know what sort of stimulant he took. Because it is impossible for a man who is correctly fed as nature wants, to have such low and destructive ideas.

Following the same thread of ideas, it might be interesting to ask what do the people who commit genocides eat. Isn't it in Rwanda that a terrible genocide was perpetrated in the 1990's? A TV program said that the people were starving. To endure this condition, they took hallucinogenic plants. Certainly, the reason why they behave so crazily and bloodthirstily.

I am convinced that there would not be any murder or war if our cells were not so deficient, excited, and poisoned. I will not go any farther with this, even if I am amazingly interested.

For the moment, let us see whether we belong to the colloidal or crystalloid type?

Besides our culinary preferences, which will most surely reveal our nature, and the first elimination crises that we had in our childhood, let us meet our "ground".

Like the colloidal types,

- **do we need a lot of time to make up our decisions?**
- **to seize the opportunities?**
- **to rather say no than yes?**

- **to be stable, loyal, perfectionist?**
- **to rarely deviate from our ideas and realizations?**
- **to be withdrawn, grumpy or resentful?**

Or like the crystalloid types,

- **do we tend to lose control and be irascible?**
- **to always be on the lookout for new ideas and enterprises?**
- **to decide and quickly seize the opportunities, sometimes too fast?**
- **to forget our encounters as soon as we leave them?**
- **to start new things but never finish them?**
- **to be early everywhere we go?**

The motto of crystalloid type persons is to go always faster, and that of the colloidal type is to have and take their time.

Knowing that we are never totally one or the other type, but **a combination of both**. If we have a good or excellent functioning, our best interest is to associate them, because far from being opposed, these two types are complementary.

Whether in a couple, in society, or in a company.

The crystalloid types are much better at opening doors to create new opportunities and colloidal types can run them better to last.

Knowing that if we do not behave correctly, we will inevitably go upside down and rather than help, we will destroy one another.

The colloidal types also build the lymphatics who enjoy and need heat, when the crystalloids will make fiery tempers who always feel hot. The first ones cicatrize slowly, sometimes very slowly, if this is not an opportunity for their body to expel the toxins, when the second will cicatrize much faster. Those examples to show that, even if quite simplified, these tempers can be easily differentiated by their strengths and respective qualities, that will turn into weaknesses as their condition becomes pathological.

Would you like to read some examples of everyday life to fully understand the incidence of food on our personality and behavior? Like this diabetic, although he never drank alcohol, who went into a terrible rage at the end of a family lunch, for no reason.

His daughters saying that he was like that each time he eats a sweet dessert.

I have observed that industrial sugar can influence the fragile cells of children, like alcohol does to adults' cells.

This young lady in her twenties who used to fall into despair every time she had too much chocolate, coffee, and cigarettes, will not deny it. Too bad that we do not link together what we ate with the way we behave consequently.

How could I forget these Easter vacations at our friends' in the mountains, where, as it is the custom, the Easter Bunny had brought quantities of chocolate hens and eggs, that the children enjoyed. Julie, my granddaughter, who was 4 years old, like the other kids, had not left her share.

But sometime after, when the other kids, who were accustomed to eating treats, were not bothered, Julie went into a terrible anger and said, as an excuse, once she had calmed down:

> ***"It is not my fault Granny, there were naughty thoughts hurting my head".***

Poor darling, that our unconsciousness had forced into that state. Like every time we offer treats to our kids, they start fighting and crying.

It made me write, one Christmas day, that King Herod was not dead, and that, to kill our children, he now came his arms full of little Jesus, sweets and chocolate of all shapes and colors, that destroy their nervous system, the foundation of their balance and happiness.

Multiple memories testify of these facts. Like this cake that one Sunday, I had bought for a doctor friend of mine. On my advice, she had swapped her trousers, used to hide her ugly varicose veins, for more feminine skirts. After two years of treatment, including a food transition, she could proudly show her legs again.

As her kids and her preferred to eat fruits, which I appreciated, once they had left, I stayed alone with the cake which I, in some ways still enjoyed. As I had bought it, I could not help tasting it, and eat another bite, then another, and another until I had eaten half of it.

I had really enjoyed it!
But what a night! What a terrible night!

At two in the morning, I woke up, sweating and scared, in this new house where I had moved a few months ago, without being ever frightened before. Any sound seemed suspect, hardly daring to breathe, I was imagining the worse horrors, until I could finally stretch my arm to turn the light on and realize the awful influence that this sugar had had on my poor cells, totally disused from that sort of poison.

I could write a whole book with similar stories, and you too, perhaps, if you knew how to link what you swallowed with the state in which you are a while after.

But, as at these moments, we are captured by dark, crazy, freaky, negative, distressing, and destructive ideas, we cannot realize it and think that it is for any reason but the right one.

How could I forget Marianne? My adorable stepsister who, when she was 15, was strongly constipated, and was also as reserved and anxious as it is possible. As her parents were divorced, this was linked to the family situation and she was sent to the hospital for some investigation. When she came out, her only prescription was to eat as much as she wanted. Her mom, of course, did her best in that sense. But since Marianne was constipated, she could not eliminate. It was normal that she refused food. And, since her excited cells could only connect her to low and inverted frequencies, **she spent her time drinking tea. The excitement gave her the illusion to have energy and then she smoked to calm down the excitement**.

This awful duet soon led her to a psychiatric hospital from which she came out a few months later, to go back again sometime after, and leave again, and then go to another one. And it lasted almost ten years. **Until the day, when she was medically healed, she came out from the hospital, and took her own life.**

Still knowing nothing about the consequences of our physiological state on our psychological and mental behavior, I just wept over little Marianne, whose sad story showed me, a long time after, the cruel indecency of our ignorance about the laws of life.

Shall I not mention the story of my last coffee? I had not drunk this beverage for years, when I had one sip from a friend's cup. A few moments after, I did a really delirious crisis, where I could have done anything, and this is not an empty word. As you can guess, since that day, I never swallowed a drop of coffee, that I now consider a real poison, and one of the most common causes of nervous breakdowns.

You maybe think that I exaggerate, so please tell me why the great coffee drinkers are so negative, and why among them there are so many suicidal people? And on the contrary, why people who do not drink it, neither alcohol, show, despite their apparent misery, so much happiness?

Give them meat, industrial sugar, tea, coffee, and alcohol and they will experience all troubles and sicknesses.

Somewhat identical, weren't these apparently insignificant elements, the same that attacked the poor cells of the people described as "possessed" 2000 years ago, whom Jesus healed with fasting, enema and prayer?

"Their excretions burnt so terribly that no grass could grow anymore..." Can we read in The Essene Gospel of Peace.

Which leaves no doubt on the acidic nature of the liquids in which these poor people's cells were plunged, leaving them drift into dementia that religions in those days called "demons".

In our technological times, how can we not dream of a device that would tell us, as with all existing wavelength measurements, that it is absolutely necessary to be connected to low and destructive frequencies in order to commit all the nonsense, madness, violence and cowardice that we are doing?

A device, that would prove us that only states generated by low frequencies can create conflicts, break-ups, borders, or frontiers that separate people, families, villages, races, classes, nations, for years, generations and centuries. A machine that would technically show us, as we have not still understood, that, in order to live in happiness, peace, positive and in a creative way, we need to be linked to the frequencies of life. These frequencies allow us in all circumstances, to find the right attitude to solve our problems, to communicate with others and combine our skills for the sake of everyone, as life seems to invite us.

But yet, in order to communicate, first of all, we have to be able to talk.

And this is not an easy task for a colloidal type person, whose cells are slowed down by the magma in which they are. This type of person is unable to express what he feels deep inside. As well as a crystalloid type whose excitement cannot stop the fast flow of words.

This reverse behavior leads both types of persons into misunderstanding and create dissensions, conflicts, or wars, that happen inside of us as well or within families, neighborhoods, between religions or states. War, that in the name of God or love or any ideology, will only spread terror and desolation everywhere.

So many human lives, energy and means have been lost to win wars!

And since to make war there needs to be two,

if we are violently attacked or despoiled, there are still two possible attitudes:

- 1/ either answer equally or even in a worse manner
- 2/ or step back and find the strength to talk to the enemy, who, feeling understood and considered, might review his position in the interest of both.

Because there never was and will never be any "good" war.

This demoniac manifestation, in addition to the destruction of the strongest men sent into battle, having entrusted the marvelous care of reproduction to the weakest persons or to those who hid themselves from going to war.

Leading to the degeneration of the strongest constitutions. The vigorous buddies slowly but certainly, swapped their joy, their consciousness, their courage, and strength, for negativity, unconsciousness, violence, and weakness of the following generations with the same constitution, that we now call lesional or chronic type.

A wonderful gift

Yes, a wonderful gift! Yes, even if life, in its splendor, gave us a wonderful gift, that, under the influence of fear and ignorance from the laws of life, we call childhood disease.

Let us remember that as soon as our body recover a little more energy than required to accomplish its daily routine, it will use it to restore its balance.

How?

By taking the risk of repeating myself, simply by getting free from the heritage that our genitors gave us by birth. This task being extremely demanding in terms of energy for a toddler's body, he will be feverish, grumpy, and tired. In my young days, we used to say that he "was coming down with something".

What to do then?

- **Either understand the role of this liberating process, and let the child's body achieve it, in order to re-generate.**
- **Or, with the intension to cure him the way we learnt, prevent his body to eliminate toxins, and force them back into his deepest layers.**

The more our cells stay in a poisoned environment, the more they like it and ask for the substance that make the poison in which they live. So, we continue to enjoy and consume this substance, and of course, to be intoxicated.

Until the day when, thanks to Spring's pollens, hay and buds' energy, our body will try again its elimination process. It means that our kids' hay fever and bronchitis are necessary crises to expel their mucus and viscosities. Their otitis, "red sicknesses", and fevers are made to eliminate their acidic loads.

Shall we treat it as it should, or call it allergy or any other illness wording that we will fight in good conscience, not realizing that we do exactly the contrary of what should be done?

Let us remember that, to go back into the blood stream that will eliminate them, guiding them to the urines and perspiration, the tiny uric acid crystals must turn from solid to liquid state. This transformation will reveal their acidic nature, making fever, pain or burn.

The strongest the children will be, the more violent and acute will their "illnesses" express, and consequently, the more medicated they will be, causing their defense system to weaken. This is why if their otitis, rhinitis, bronchitis disappear, they will be replaced by allergies, eczema, or psychological and mental problems. These crises being no longer functional nor lesional illnesses.

The art of fighting against a disease has nothing to see with that of protecting and improving health.

Because the crises or illnesses "properly healed" in the western medicine sense, can cause tremendous harm.

I randomly, pick up the example of this tall and good looking forty years old man, who was President of his town's epileptic community when I met him. I investigated on his child diseases, as I always do, when I learnt that, aged of a few months, he suffered from a strong diarrhea (functional crisis) that led him to the hospital where he was rapidly cured. He went back again the year after with convulsions (attempt of a functional crisis with a lesional tendency) and was as rapidly "healed", having a strong constitution.

This type of "healing" consisting, let us make no mistake about it, in "unplugging" the child's elimination system who, not being able to eliminate, will seem cured.

Initially, this seems true, but as soon as little François had recovered enough energy, he used it once more for another attempt to remove the poisoned load that he had inherited and was concealed in his "humors".

His, being particularly acidic.

His tired and exhausted kidneys having a hard time trying to eliminate, his little body tried to drag out the loads from their depth. They invaded his cerebral and nervous cells, provoking a delirium which is the first manifestation of all urinary difficult crisis, and that we call epilepsy (a lesional crisis). This task requiring a lot of energy, François's little body had to mute all the functions that were not essential to achieve the elimination process.

Provoking a coma, which is the second step in an epilepsy crisis.

It would only end when François' weakened kidneys would be able to eliminate, that is to pee. The symptomatic medicine, with which he was treated, mastering the art of turning off the red lights, his epileptic crises miraculously disappeared. Thinking he was cured, he went to college, became an engineer, got married and had a little girl.

Everything was fine until one day, his epileptic crises came back, more violent than ever, and did not respond to any treatment. Refusing to impose his 7 to 8 crises per night to his wife and daughter, with a heavy heart, he decided to break up.

For the best or the worse, the years went by until we met. **When after four months of treatment, yes, four months, not one more, his seven to eight comas per night had turned down to a half one which intensity had also decreased.**

Simply because, fed with vegetable, like he should always have been, his organism did not need this renal pressure to eliminate the acidic and congenital overload that his childhood diarrhea, his first epilepsy crises and convulsions, had tried to eject out of his body.

François is just a case among others!

Let us take a look at Marie. She, too, had fevers, otitis, bronchitis in her youth. All were attributed to germs, cold, heat, emotional problems, and treated the classical way. Which turned this strong and beautiful child into a fragile and delicate girl who needed, as recommended, to be well fed.

But eat what?

The fruits and vegetables that her little intoxicated body refused?
Or the yoghurts, ham, veal liver and animal brains supposed to fortify her body, and that she liked so much.

Which, besides the medical treatments, made her suffer not only from functional crises she already knew, but also from lesional crises, and more exactly epilepsy crises, which, treated the classical way, transformed this child with great artistic and intellectual capacities, into a nervous, disturbed and erratic person.

Surprising?
No, but the opposite should be.

Let us forget these epileptics for other regrettable consequences, which ensue from this way of feeding and treating our kids. Let us first take a glance at these two little girls whose father, a doctor, had them treated only by top doctors, to stop the many fevers and ear infections that they had in their early childhood. It turned these adorable girls with an anorexic tendency, into rather plump adolescents, which pleased their parents who were so happy to see them eat.

But eat what?
Fruits and veggies?

Not at all!

They preferred the creams and pastries that their mom cooked so well, and also the cheese and meat supposed to strengthen them.
This type of food, poor in active nutrients but rich in residues, could only raise their toxemia and exhaust their organism. So, at the age of fifteen they weighed respectively 255 and 275 pounds (115 and 125 kg).

Their parents took them to see the best weight-loss nutritionists. Instead of giving them vegetable juices and fruits that they needed the most, they prescribed them protein and even ultra-protein diet. It intoxicated them ever more, saturating their worn urinary system, that started to retain liquids, making them swell up always more.

Not so bad?

Simply ask them, when they spend most of their time and parents' money, to cook and eat, become slaves of their inverted taste.

Ask them again, when, already handicapped by their overweight and its consequently loss of mobility, they have to breathe outside every five minutes, even in Winter, to soothe the inner fire lit by their accumulated acids.

Is not that a sort of hell?

If not, it looks like it. And we did not mention the embarrassment caused by this situation, either in their relationships or their work, as well as for their parents, who do not know what to do to save them from this situation.

Obesity, like epilepsy, can only be treated efficiently and sustainably, by following the laws of life.

Incidentally, we can easily see that among wild animals there are no more epileptics than obese. Just like among the people who eat according to the laws of nature. Whereas these two diseases grow exponentially in our civilized world.

A quick glance at the United Stated is enough to confirm.

Where hamburgers, popcorn, and sodas have, in a minimum time, transformed the population in real overweight or obese persons, whom, for some of them, cannot even walk through the doorway. And all this, while another part of humanity in the third world, is starving. This sad and unfair repartition of goods is no advantage, for any part.

Because dying from starvation or from obesity, is always dying. And the pains of the ones, are equal to those if the others.
Another good reason to think about what we eat if we want to have nice shapes and remain in a good vitality.

As habits build laws, we are far from imagining how deplorable consequences our nutritional and therapeutic errors impose on our dear little children.

One day, a beautiful lady came to my office. Staring at her carefully, I was asking myself what the reason of her venue could be, when, taking off her wig, she showed a totally bald skull.

Answering my usual questions, she mentioned having had many strong fevers when she was a child, and at the age of three, she had been saved from a serious illness.

Considering her nice and strong constitution, I could easily imagine the violence of this crisis as well as the doctor's and her parents' panic. It was also easy to understand that, not being evacuated, her abundant crystals remained at the surface of her skin where, lacking of energy to go through, and being unresponsive to any of the treatments that they received, they simply burned her hair roots, her body hair and eyelashes.

It is not the only case that I met. There are many more than one could imagine. But with a nice wig, you could not tell. I saw several times, with children or teenagers having a weaker constitution, that this hair loss was often doubled with eczema and nervous disorders.

Can hair grow again?

Let us ask this man who had been wearing a wig for 17 years and came to see me for another reason. After eighteen months of treatment, he was surprised to see his hair grow again. They were not of the best quality though, but they were back and continued to grow stronger so that he could leave his wig.

The consequences of our dietary and therapeutic errors are so many that I cannot mention them all. Still, how not to talk about Veronique, this lovely 18-month little girl, treated with the classical medicines for her frequent fevers, that not only stopped her fever but her sleep as well. Veronique had not slept for months and was miserably whining in her parents' arms when they brought her.
Two months of reform and dietary supplements, without forgetting baths and essential oils to calm down and fortify her nervous system, and she recovered, as well as her parents and grand-parents who came to help, the simple and immense pleasure of sleeping.

The acidic residues that the fevers had tried to drag out in vain, had totally consumed the indispensable minerals for the nervous system. In that condition, being unable to sleep was quite normal.

Before we leave this chapter, let us talk about this ski and canoe teacher who came for hemorrhoids and eczema, supposed to be the consequence of his wet clothes. Apparently maybe, but not in reality! Because it is impossible to have hemorrhoids and eczema on a non-intoxicated ground. Moreover, his father who had the same culinary tastes, has suffered all his life from the same affections, although he never touched water. So, treated as he had been, and continuing to eat bread, cheese and wine that go well together, his father had died, at the age of 50, from an anus cancer. Which did not prevent his son to confess that he might not be ready to change his diet.

We should be aware that it is much easier for most of us to take pills or get surgery, than change our eating habits.

Unfortunately, if he does not, he may, like his father, pay the high price. Whereas if he accepts to do the first step, the naturally live and delicious food, will quickly help his eczema and hemorrhoids disappear. But this is a personal choice, and he is the only one who can make it.

Now let us talk about Annie, a lovely young woman who came for heavy legs and varicose veins. Despite my insisting questions, she had always refused to talk about her work. Until the day when having recovered her normal legs, together with a great energy, she accepted to tell me that she was a prostitute and had decided to stop and work in the family company.

Coincidence? Of course not!

Her new behavior having linked her to some higher frequencies, she had logically decided to change her life.

Should our deficiencies and toxins have an influence on our endocrine system?

I have every reason to believe it.

Surprising consequences

Alexis Carrel, the great precursor, said that, while our food, medicine and pharmacy were progressing; health, mentality, people level of consciousness and spirituality dangerously decreased.

This doctor was not a visionary. He had simply observed that, far from improving our health, that kind of progress could, in the long term, only impair our health.

Indeed, if this improvement was as efficient as pretended, instead of having more and more hospitals and jails, we should have already closed them.

Not by lack of means, but of sick people and burglars.

But the situation is far from that!

How could it be different, when the industry only proposes food that is less and less energetic and more and more fouling?

How could it be different when, not belonging to life, these toxins are for our body like nuclear waste for our planet?

How could it be different, when, instead of helping our body to free itself each time it is necessary, we stop it?

All good reasons for, our weak and intoxicated bodies, to only be able to connect to the lowest frequencies, while these insane, torn, dark, destructive ideas invade our head and heart, giving birth to revolt, frustration, greed, hate and fear.

So many reasons that lead us reverse to common-sense, the sense of happiness and health which belong to all the beings who follow the laws of life.

So many reasons that drive us to give our offspring the diseases that are not anymore due to microbes or viruses destroyed with antibiotics. But due to our genes, intoxicated with this poisoned and poisoning flow, deeply hidden into our underground layers.

So many reasons that force us to consume more and more stimulants and medicines which, by fostering the degeneration of our children and grand-children, make them catch diseases as they are still young, that our grand-parents only got once they were old.

We all heard of some old person coughing all night long, obliged to sleep seated not to suffocate.

Doesn't it look like the cystic fibrosis of our kids nowadays?

Not a painful ailing in the full sense of the term, but quite annoying and affecting more and more young children who have to remain their head bent downward a great part of their lives not to suffocate.

Did we ever ask ourselves where this mucus came from, so that we could prevent them? Or did we just give antibiotics to our children, to stop them from coughing and spitting each time they endure a respiratory affection?

Locking down ever deeper the mucus that their little bodies were trying to evict and continuing to feed them with pasta and fries they love.

Their bodies cannot free them from these sticky and viscous matters but with drugs and clapping.

When this mother called, to ask me if I could take care of her 16 years old daughter who had been suffering from cystic fibrosis since she was 6 and had serious chronic bronchitis since, I was not surprised to hear that her daughter's favorite food was:
wheat mush with sweet concentrated milk every morning, lunch, and dinner.

That sounded impossible! But to me that was normal, because the more we are intoxicated, the more we are addicted to this food. I just told her to replace the mush with vegetable soups, fruits, fresh or in puree, which, if not totally the best, significantly improved her condition.

It did not mean that she was totally healed, far from it indeed. Because the better she would eat the more her body would use this energy to expel the lyophilized and reduced toxemia that had been locked in her for years and even before her birth.

This would require a long and important work.

This way of seeing things was not accepted by her doctors. They proposed a lungs transplant. Her parents joyfully accepted with gratitude. And moreover, their daughter would be able to eat everything she wanted did they say triumphantly.

In the first times, this was true, "same causes giving same effects", it is most likely that her exhausted liver will continue to produce loads of viscosities which again, will invade her lungs, if she keeps on with her favorite diet.

This is why I said that, if ever a surgery should be done,

it should be consolidated with a non-colloidal diet.

But our medicine is still not aware of this.

Which means that since all the cases of cystic fibrosis have the same origin, it is an obligation to start replacing the carbohydrates that these people love, with veggies and cooked food in the first place, followed by a more and more raw and alive diet.

As you easily understand, this is essential for their recovery.

We all remember an old person who rambled and "fell back into childhood" as she was aging.

Doesn't it sound like today's autism, or to the ADHD (Attention Deficit Hyperactivity Disorder) so common in the United States?

Science only proposes to lock these persons down under surveillance, where they will spend the rest of their lives.

Because if it is rather easy for the conventional medicine to "cure", that is to stop functional crises; it cannot so easily stop the lesional ones and is almost unable to stop, that is to heal, the degenerative or genetic illnesses which, in all good faith it contributed to create.

During a television show on April 1, 1994 presented by Jean Marie CAVADA, Mrs. LAXXSER explained that her son Jerome, had an encephalitis when he was 9 months old, and that he was rapidly "cured" with classical methods. She also mentioned that a few months later, her son did not have the same behavior. He seemed sleepy and his growth slowed down.

Following which Jerome had all sorts of examination and was declared autist.

Do we have to mention that the doctor recommended the mother to leave him in some specialized institution, where he would seem to feel well?

As we mentioned several times, the "healing" of this child's encephalitis, the way it was done, had retained his toxemia, deeply inside his underground layers. His cerebral liquids being overloaded, **the cerebral and nervous transmissions were slowed down and diverted**.

Indeed, we can easily observe that almost all the autistic children got sick after a powerful disease which, well cured by the western medicine, ended by locking down the viscosities trying to escape from their brain.

Don't we read in the French encyclopedia "Le Larousse", that well treated encephalitis is often followed by mental troubles? Or other troubles, like the impotence of this boy, treated for an encephalitis when he was 18 months, and who became impotent as he turned adult.

Not a big deal?

Go and ask him when married to the girl he loves since his childhood, she found someone else to have the baby that he could not give her. Also ask him, why the only ideas that came to his mind to soothe him were to sink into alcohol?

Who made the link between his encephalitis supposedly cured, and his wasted life?

Who realized that the residues of this encephalitis had gone to his genital endocrines to provoke his adulthood impotence?

But is this so important, when science pretends to have solutions for all our problems, proposing artificial fertilization or genetic manipulations, to clone as many “super beings” as we wish?

But until this fabulous and scientific masterpiece, we can see that the little premature babies born out of artificial fertilization, can weigh less than 1.65 pound (0.750 kg) and can arrive by several at the same time, just like animals whose species is endangered.

This may be less disturbing than not having any baby at all. But still, ask them if they wouldn’t have preferred to have them one by one instead of five at a time?

The reason is simple, and we know it.

We cannot continue to play with the laws of life the way we do. Even if progress convinced us that vaccination is enabled to protect us from illness, without wondering what our body would do with its poisoned and poisoning overloads, that the vaccine stopped from being expelled out of our bodies

What will it do?

We know it now. It will hide them in our deep layers. More and more intoxicated, they will push us to consume the poisoning food in which our cells bathe.

And each time our body tries to excrete them, it stops and buries them deeper inside.

Until one day, they reach, deteriorate, sclerose or de-program our genes.

Thus, slowly but surely, occur the fourth-class diseases, that we skillfully name genetic diseases. And we still refuse to ask ourselves why these genetic programs that have transmitted the information through thousands or millions of generations, suddenly deteriorate.

How can we believe such a senseless thing?

To properly understand what happened, let us simply look back, when we started to be vaccinated against smallpox that has now disappeared. So happy with the perspective of progress, 20 or 25 years later, we did not have smallpox anymore, this other way to eliminate toxins by the skin, dairies, and charcuteries that we were fed with. Instead we got typhoid fever, liberating us from the acidic load that our weakened immune system had not been able to push through the skin barriers.

Typhoid fever being a lesional crisis for which we have been vaccinated.

Once this disease also disappeared, the following generations got poliomyelitis, a deeper crisis that the weaker defense system could almost never manage, and against which, once again, we have been vaccinated. And what happened when polio disappeared?

We got "myopathy"!

This succession of illnesses means that in less than a century, and under the triumphant banner of progress and science, we have replaced the functional and liberating crises of our strong ancestors, by lesional crises.

Treated as we do, they will turn into degenerative illnesses, that will become, after a little time of "good care", not simple elimination crises, but real genetic illnesses.

Shall we dream of a vaccine and offer with a "Telethon", a wheel chair or another alleviating means to the victims of this inverted world, or can we remember our "good-sense" and learn how **to make healthy children, free and happy, as life wants?**

The question is asked.
Each one can think about
it and find his own answer!

Knowing that it depends on us and only on us, to have strong and healthy children.

Happy children who will become sound, optimistic and creative adolescents, women, and men, growing older with a rich and wise experience useful to others.

Shall we understand, or shall we continue to be unconscious and drink, eat, care like progress tells us?

And when we retire have a heart attack, embolism, cerebral hemorrhage, or aneurism, putting an early end to our journey on Earth, or leaving us crippled in a wheelchair until the end.

Or maybe attacked by our "dear toxemia", our cells will cause nervous motor seizures like Parkinson, multiple sclerosis, or another paralysis.

Or as it is often the case, they reach our cells' brain, trying to continue their task, this time not for the sake of all as they did until then, but for themselves, in total anarchy.

I am talking about "cancer". Depending on our constitution and other criteria, it will be a breast, prostate, uterus cancer, or any other part of the body; but whose root cause will still be the same. Sad fatality, shall we whisper, forgetting that analyzing and treating the consequences of our inconsistent behaviors without modifying anything, could lead to nothing else.

Cancer, like other diseases, is only the consequence of our multiple errors.

Moreover, it is not through fighting the way we do, that we will free ourselves, but rather by rebuilding our energy, so that our body eliminates its toxins the same way they came in.

Dozens of practice years have told me that cancer patients have the best chances to recover until they receive the heavy treatments or classical medicine. Because even if it is sometimes necessary, let us not forget that it weakens the defense system. So, it will be harder for the patient to free from his toxemia.

As it was the case for this man in his fifties, who suffered from a prostate cancer and had eight chemotherapies and as many perfectly well-made surgeries. Having no more solution for him, the classical medicine sent him back home to wait for the end. This is when his wife, refusing to wait without trying anything, decided to come and see me.

What could I do in such conditions?

The treatments had damaged his immune system so much that when a crisis would appear, I knew that he would be unable to bear it, and that would be the end.

I was going to refuse the case, when she asked me to just give him hope, not to feel abandoned. That expression of her humanity moved me, and I decided to go and give him a nutritional program every week and some dietary supplements. I found him paralyzed and under morphine.

After two months of treatment he did not suffer anymore and quit morphine. The energy was coming back.

Was he healed? Not at all!

I knew that as soon as his body would have enough energy, he would attempt to expel its toxins. So, I was not so confident. And so, it did, with an abscess near the anus. That was certainly the shortest way that nature had found to get rid of its prostatic residues. The abscess turned red, swelled, and despite my pessimistic expectations. I started to hope. But as I predicted, the medical treatments had totally destroyed his defense system. So, he was unable to take this abscess to maturity and never went back to his factory. We had been really close. I kept thinking that with, maybe two or three less chemotherapies, his strong constitution might have driven the abscess to maturity and start a real healing. I never told his wife and daughters, who were happy anyway to keep him and care for him a bit longer until his last sigh.

Does this mean that medical treatments are evil?

This is not exactly what I mean

But as we all know, **these treatments are only meant to destroy the infected cells, without protecting the healthy ones**. This is why, even if it sometimes good to remove an organ or a tumor, we must realize that these surgeries never modify the ground, and this sole technique will never help to recover a good health.

Should we then refuse any type of medication?

No of course. Especially when it is necessary, like for degenerative illnesses. And also, because when the house is burning, you call the firemen, Pierre Valentin Marchesseau used to say.

This is not the role of the naturopathic practitioner, whose aim is to prevent the house from burning, to limit the damage in case of fire, and, when it is possible, the ones created by the firemen while extinguishing the fire.

This means that allopathic medicine is a medicine of emergency. The best would be to combine all the medical techniques and methods which can help to save a sick person, as it was the case for Sylvie, an excellent illustration of what I am saying.

Sylvie was eighteen months when I laid my eyes on her, in the waiting room where her parents were sitting. They did not come for her, but for themselves. Yet, when I saw her, the word "leukemia" immediately came to my mind, as if a little voice had told me. I asked her parents to take her back home in bed and to wait until I call them.

I was devastated and did not know what to do. I went back to my office to think and ask for help to this sublime life intelligence.

Suddenly came the idea to call my young daughter in law, who was a resident in pediatrics. Surprised by my attitude she asked me to take the child to the hospital for some examination. The team she was working with spent the whole night on her.

At around 6 in the morning they told me that **Sylvie had an acute leukemia of the worst type, and that, according to medical records, she had two or three months to live**.

As I had never had such a case, I called my naturopathic school for some advice. They ordered me to leave the child into the hospital's hands and to support her by all possible means.

Which was accepted by the hospital's head of service, saying that since the baby was lost, there was nothing to fear.

Sylvie received the emergency treatment, snuggled in her bed as if waiting for her death, that no-one was ready to accept. Following my indications, her parents fed her exclusively with beetroot juice, carrots, parsley, apples and grape freshly pressed in a syringe, with some crushed dietary supplement corresponding to her age.

Believing in this superior force called God, her parents organized a prayer chain, and every day the little girl received a hands-on-healing treatment and some gentle massage with essential oils diffused in her room.

Two long months passed until Sylvie started to wake up. And another month when she went out of the hospital in the triumphing arms of her father, who still continued to take her once a week for medical controls.

Sylvie's parents followed the treatment to the letter, including mine, and it was a real moment of happiness to witness her healing. Her complexion had the color of the apricot. Her energy and joy of living looked like a miracle.

Still, after some time, it seemed that her weekly treatment caused her over-fatigue and I asked her parents to mention it to the doctor. It seemed to me that emergency medicine having done its job, she only needed revitalization.

But what to do, when parents and doctors believing in the benefit of the medical treatment, refuse to stop it?

We were going nowhere, and I did not know what else to say, when the little 2 years old girl who was never capricious nor bad-tempered, suddenly refused to go to the hospital where she was always warmly welcome.

She did such a rage at the door, rearing back and stretching with all her strength, that her parents had to take her back home.

So, I continued to treat Sylvie who was getting always better and becoming a splendid girl. Her beautiful black hair that had fallen with the chemotherapy, grew again. The inner envelope of her eyes was bright red and she was as heavy as lead.

All signs showing that her health was strongly rebuilding and that she still possesses 15 years after.

Shall I mention that, to the great surprise of her doctors, the examinations that they did 8 months later, left no tracks of her illness.

Isn't Sylvie's healing a wonderful story?

A healing that medicine or naturopathy alone would never have seen, not ignoring the immense faith of her parents.

How, after that, not dream of a really new medicine, a sort of "integrative medicine", able to bring together the know-how and knowledge of all the parties who, in conscious, work to help the patients recover their health and well-being.

From our inconsistencies

I wanted to also talk about Jeff, whom I chose for this sad indictment.

As a little child, he used to have fever reaching 102 to 104°F (39 or 40°C) each week, said his father who called the doctor for some recently discovered penicillin. Since each time it decreased, the fever came back after a few days, Jean-François ("Jeff") received a range of penicillin's treatments. He had a difficult time to reach his third year when, after having his tonsil and adenoids removed, the fever seemed to end.

Still, his father noticed that he was unable to walk along a curb or go down the stairs without falling. All sorts of investigations were made and found a scoliosis that all physiotherapies could not improve.

Of course! Because coming from the inside, it could not be treated from the outside.

It was decided then to put a plaster cast around him. And among other inconveniences, the family had to leave the beautiful apartment they had just bought, for a ground floor house, so that he could go out with his wheelchair.

A few years went by, and despite all the efforts the scoliosis worsened, making a hump under Jean-François' left shoulder. Obviously, he was turning humpbacked!

How could this be possible in this strong Burgundy family?

Hazard, bad luck, fatality were invoked; not realizing that to decrease his fever, his little body had each time, been forced to stop the elimination process, where he obstinately tried to expel the millions of crystals that his forebearers had transmitted to him by birth. The reason why his body had created this ultimate dump.

It did not prevent Jean-François from becoming an engineer and spend most of his spare time cooking one of those good meals he liked to enjoy with his friends. Everyone getting used to the situation, until a few years after, every four steps, Jean-François had to lift up his leg to walk. His ever-growing toxemia had evolved so much, that it had reached his motor cells. They restarted the investigations concluding to hydrocephaly. He consulted the best doctors who decided to open his skull and divert the excess liquids to the digestive tract. The surgeon having promised to Jean-François that following the surgery he would be cured. He did not hesitate between this promising solution and the treatment that I proposed, which was not as optimistic, but only expected to end the worsening and get some slow but constant improvements.

So, the surgery was done, but the results were not as expected...

Quite confident, the surgeon did it a second time, with another failure. He tried a third and a fourth operation, without improving anything. And the poor boy had to return to the wheelchair of his childhood.

And he left this world in terrible pain, much too early.

Let us now see Alexis, this 5-year-old boy, who arrived one day like a tornado at my office where he swept down everything on my desk, in a single gesture. Staggered, I searched for his mother's eyes, who told me that this was one of the reasons why she took him to me.

Butcher, son of butcher, his father had just left his wife and son, not bearing him anymore. I learnt through the child's health investigation that he suffered from three otitis during his first year. If the two first ones had been healed, the last one had necessitated a paracentesis, after which the mother thought that her son could not hear anymore. The doctor tried to reassure her, and the examinations showed an almost total deafness.

Surprising?
No, it is the contrary that should be!

The residues that his otitis could not eliminate had remained in his auditory canal, deprived of any sound. Locked down is this deep silence, the child could not reproduce the sounds that he no more heard and became mute.

When he arrived at my office, his audiometric test was 96,01%, which means that he was almost totally deaf. After 18 months of treatment, his next test showed 40,81%, showing than more that 50% of his audition capacity were recovered.

Moreover, he had greatly improved his behavior, surprising his schoolteacher who had ruined her holidays at the idea of having him in her class the following semester.

Alexis is not the only one in this case. It is common to see deaf and mute children, declared so by birth, who actually became disabled after a strong child disease, supposedly well-treated as we know. Like it was for Julia's grandmother, who became deaf after a serious bronchopneumonia. Deaf and of course mute, she leaved in a specialized institution, where she met the one who was to become her husband. And who, like her, had become deaf and mute in the same condition.

Many people also became blind after a serious child disease.

I do not mean, of course, that we should not treat our children when they are ill. Of course not, but we should learn how to treat them correctly, to avoid all these catastrophes.

Teach their little body how to relieve from the miserable heritage that we gave them, rather than lock it down as we do.

Shall I also mention Benoit, this nice and strong 6 years old boy. Following the advice of Maguy Lebrun, the author of "Médecins du Ciel et de la Terre" (ndt: "Doctors from Earth and Heaven"), his grandmother asked me to go and see him at the hospital of Marseille. Knowing that his broken immune system would not drive any crisis to its term, I was to refuse.

Still, perfectly conscious of the risks, I went. It was hot, really hot in the aseptic room where, armed with pipes, he was playing with the water from the sink.

He had been at the hospital for 8 months, under heavy treatment.

But why was he there?

The previous Autumn, he fell down, after what he practically lost the use of his legs. Some examinations revealed a small tumor on the bump's site. It was removed and he recovered the use of his legs. But further investigations showed a marrow cancer.

How could this be possible?

Once again, all this was quite logical. When he was very young, Benoit had suffered from many illnesses that his godfather, freshly graduated from Medical University, had conscientiously treated. He, then, buried the heavy toxic heritage that the child's body was trying to eliminate, and which silently ravaged the boy.

Differently from his brother who loved fruits, Benoit liked only charcuteries, canned sardines, and everything that was bad for him; showing us that kid's taste is not only due to education.

Just arriving at the hospital, I examined with no leniency, the sterile room with its repulsive chemical smell, wondering how it could be possible to heal people in such an atmosphere.

And also, how could one believe in a beneficial effect of long-term radio- and chemotherapies, which destroyed more healthy cells than they killed sick cells. Moreover, without ever changing anything to what had provoked this state.

Of course, these treatments weakened the defense and regeneration abilities of the cells. In such a nonsense, I thought of **Mirko Beljanski**, a scientific researcher at the Pasteur Institute, who had recently found a way to protect the healthy cells treated by classical medicine. Not promoted as we could believe, he had freshly been dismissed.

He was told that the financial report of a cancer or AIDS patient, was not to be discussed. How in such conditions not to wonder who is making a fool of us, moreover when one still begs for medical research donations?

What sort of research, sorry?

The one that improves patients' life and health, or the one that fired a scientist who made such a discovery?

Would it be the liter of marrow that was pumped out of Benoit's back to make a transplant - and which was never used - or the barbaric and useless treatments that he received that would heal him?

Or maybe could it be the mashed potatoes, the burnt sausage, and the yoghourt he was brought?

I was mad as hell, seeing this food whose only advantage was to be sterile. Sterile, but dead, totally dead, without any energy, that was sure.

Feeling the rebellion growing into me, I thought that "He" was really malevolent, to let us believe that so unnatural stuff could ever heal us. And I started imagining Benoit lying under the plane trees that shaded the family home and suggested it to his mother, who was staying with him since he had arrived at the hospital. She thought of it and told herself that there was nothing to lose, since he was in a terminal state. And three days later, they were back home.

It was wonderful to see Benoit build a hut under the trees. A whole bunch of happiness and everyone started to hope. Me too, although I knew that but with a miracle, as soon as his body would have more energy, he would try another elimination crisis that he could not achieve and that would be the end. Exactly like it happened on that beautiful sunny day, his whole family surrounding him, his little hand in mine, when

I felt the weak current still animating him flow away. Benoit had just passed. Not even 6 years old.

And within them, 9 months of suffering Isn't that hell?

Benoit had gone. Let us now talk about Philippe who was not yet 5 when his grandparents brought him to me. He was shaking his head heavily from one shoulder to the other, while his trembling hands were desperately trying to seize the telephone.

Undressing him I was shocked by a strong odor of urine, although he was absolutely clean. This revealed that he was totally overloaded with acids. I asked as usual about his childhood's illnesses to know which one brought the most important toxins, and which were the systems that nature had chosen to eliminate them. As a toddler, Philippe had several high fevers and convulsions. It destroyed the minerals of his bone structure, which explained that he could not stand with his head up.

We had to clear his little body from all the acids that were drowned in him, so that the minerals that I prescribed, could remain in his body. I established his treatment in this sense, plus two hot baths per day, with aromatic plants to help his perspiration, that his grandfather would collect in the surrounding scrubland.

No need to say that I replaced the animal proteins with a maximum of fruits, raw vegetables and as many vegetable fresh juices, rich in minerals, that he could drink.

The progress was spectacular

After two months, he was able to seize the telephone and say a few intelligible words. His grandparents were overjoyed, me too, and after 8 months of treatment, Philippe smelt lavender, thyme, and rosemary. He was able to stand up and walk on his own.

Seeing him better, his mother took him back home, but without continuing the treatment. The same cause giving the same effects, all the progresses that Philippe had made disappeared and 2 years later he was placed in a specialized institution. Mad about that, his grandparents could do nothing against the law, and only got him back 8 years later.

But fed and treated the classic way, his body was totally petrified and paralyzed. God knows that he had received many animal proteins, drugs, and surgeries.

The last one, on his back, to finally paralyze him.

His grandmother, who had all the difficulties moving this big boy from his bed recently told me:

"He is more flexible since he has been eating as you recommend"

This is alas, all what we can expect now. I still continue to think that if the treatment we had started had not been interrupted, Philippe might have grown up normally.

Let us now, talk about Florence who was 9 years old when dribbling, with dazed bulging eyes, her mom brought her in her wheelchair. She too bent her head from one shoulder to the other and had been saved from a severe illness.

While talking to her, I saw a flash of intelligence and happiness, in the dull look of the girl. Hopeful, I proposed a treatment that overcame our expectations. Florence, who had a beautiful constitution, regained energy incredibly quickly. Sometime later, as expected, she had a strong bronchitis with high fever, that we treated my way.

Her crisis barely finished, to her parents' surprise she asked for her tricycle. We were in December and that sounded rather unusual. And that was not all, Florence standing straight, pedaled for three hours, as she had never done. Her progress continued, each time better after each crisis, until she no more dribbled. Her gazing became livelier and more precise. She started to talk more clearly and surprised her educators in the institution where she went each day with the meals and dietary supplements that her mother brought.

Two years passed when the young adolescent started to work on her computer with a lot of interest. She had an incredible vitality, but her twisted backbone, coiled like an S, dangerously shrunk her respiratory capacities. I proposed that she see a surgeon who could correct her spine with an articulated device, as they do, and it was a success.

Although this back paralysis leaves her forever in her wheelchair, Florence is happy and can stand straight, which is not bad and allows her lungs to fully breathe.

These examples are only a few samples of the consequences made by our inconsistencies

Very recently I met a beautiful child, who, after a gastro-enteritis just when he was born, and treated normally, became a total autist.
Yes! All these poisons that he could not evacuate, had no other possibility than invade his cerebral system. His wonderful little cells bathed in a "glue", preventing them from achieving their goal.

This means that if the medical improvements seem to have defeated the great pandemics and the functional diseases, they also, and this not as glorious, created many disabled and contributed to the development of lesional and degenerative illnesses, that constantly grow. And this does not consider the known and not yet known, genetic disorders that we will soon discover in such conditions.

AIDS

While waiting for these times, we must admit that if we are not affected by functional crises anymore, we do have lesional, degenerative illnesses and genetic affections. And moreover, all forms of violence, exclusions, madness, wars, suicidal behaviors, that expand like never before.

Is this really what we expected from progress?

Certainly not!

A TV show recently presented a new disease that develops in the United States and starts spreading over France. The children who are affected do not have one minute of rest and huge difficulties to sleep. These little kids are diagnosed as hyperactive, which is smarter than hyper excited, that they currently are. This is due to both the insane diet which feeds them, and the repressive medical treatments that they receive in all developed countries.

Whatever they are, hyperactive or hyperexcited, they are treated with amphetamines. Even if they might satisfy children, parents, professors, therapists, and pharmaceutical companies, these are well-known to be dangerous poisons.

The most commonly used among these amphetamines, says Dr Breggin, is RitalinÒ.

This is a useful medicine that rapidly soothes the children and works as an appetite suppressant since they often are bulimic. This medicine is a drug, does he insist, trying to avoid the sad consequences where it takes the children. As no-one seems to understand, it will not be surprising if new genetic diseases later appear, believed to come from the altered genes that this substance has damaged. They will be the first victims of these chain reaction errors.

If you think that I exaggerate, I am not the only one and I am proud to read that Professor Henri Joyeux, the distinguished Montpellier-based oncologist, recently wrote an article called:

"We must dare to say".

Yes, we must dare to say that it is an illusion to think that tomorrow or even after tomorrow, genetic therapies will do miracles. It has been tested in the United States of America, for the last 10 years, he wrote, without any convincing results as for now.

Like all illusions, this one will only lead us to disillusions.

It would be so simple to avoid going that far, starting with correctly feed our children.

It would prevent us from destroying their natural protection, each time their body tries to restore the balance with fever, otitis or bronchiolitis... Preferring to drive their immune system to silence when it only tries to warn us that their toxemic tolerance threshold is in the red and that it is urgent to soothe it. And since under the influence of fear and ignoring the laws of life, we force it to silence, it finally becomes mute.

Constantly pushing back the toxemia into their humors, who turn into a filthy swamp, welcoming this virus called HIV, accused of having engendered what science call Acquired Immune Deficiency Syndrome or AIDS.

It is more comfortable to say that AIDS is responsible, than the ground in which it was allowed to settle and grow.

Observation being our best teacher, it seems that all the HIV-positive persons whom I met or heard of, have a strong colloidal ground, whereas the cancer patients are rather crystalloids.

At this stage, the residues being so mixed up, the only way to be sure is to observe the dietary tastes of the patient. They will reveal with no doubt, that people with cancer love meat, while HIV-positives enjoy pasta, bread, pizza, rice, and starches which are at the origin of flus, bronchitis, asthmas, anxieties of their childhood. "Well treated", they accumulated glue and viscosities which, when they decompose, create this putrid environment that the HIV seems to appreciate.

Like any other living creature, it can only live and develop with its appropriate food. Once again, let us open up the great book of nature and imagine that we are on a mountain's brook edge, it is clear and pure water running over the stones. What are the animals that live in this ideal scenery? Now, let us imagine that we are in the sewers of Paris. What animals can we observe?

Are they the same? Of course not!

Still, both live in the same environment, water which, in one case, is particularly clean and in the other, totally dirty. This single difference allows trouts, with a pink and delicate flesh, to live in the crystal-clear water of the mountain river, and the horrible rats, or other disgusting animals, to live and grow in the dirty smelly water of the sewers.

Once again, you may find my point of view a bit simple or simplistic?

Well, try and put the trouts in the sewers and the rats in the brook and it won't be long until you realize that the trouts have lost their delicacy and the rats switch their awful and drab fur for shiny and silky hair, that now look like that of the beavers.

This make us think about the undeniable influence of food upon every living creature, from which the HIV has no reason to escape.

Don't we find many hepatic patients in some African and Asian countries, who mostly eat cooked manioc and rice? The liver, master of the sugar digestion, happily got clogged with this cooked and hydro-carbonated food, until, before he got vaccinated, its owner could periodically free himself with crises that we call "liver crisis".

And is not it to these supposed underdeveloped countries, that our laboratories and civilized nations, have generously offered a vaccine against hepatitis, whose sole objective is to stop their precious crises. Even if they are uncomfortable, their role was to evacuate the excess of mucus.

Is this so difficult to understand?

Let me tell you this little story that happened in 1990 in Geneva and that I hope, will catch your attention. Some young persons whom I knew, asked me if I could take care of one of their friends who suffered from AIDS and could not afford to pay me. I accepted to meet the young man who was in his thirties and had a good constitution.

He told me all the cold, bronchitis, and child's asthma that he got. His mother too was asthmatic when she was pregnant. He also told me about his medically treated depression when he was an adolescent and the "blues episodes" that followed. He studied art and music as a professional. Then got married and had a little girl and everything was great when he had the opportunity to work in Hollywood. He accepted and moved there, lived comfortably, when one day, a medical examination revealed he had AIDS.

A big shock of course!

Happily, his strong constitution having helped him preserve his instinct, he refused all medications. Instead, he flew to Morocco with his backpack, where he thought he could spend the rest of his life away from his wife and daughter's look, whom he wanted to preserve from seeing him decline in difficult conditions. Sleeping in a tent, he mostly ate fruits from the surrounding plantations, until one day, having recovered enough energy, he had a big abscess on his knee. Luckily, he found a Moroccan doctor who helped him with his abscess. "*It's crazy how good I felt once it ended suppurating*" he said.

He felt so well that he decided to go back to Switzerland, where, going back to the classical diet, bronchitis started again, treated by his doctor as usual.

Sad distinction, he was elected President of the AIDS Association in Geneva, and explained me he wanted to go back to Morocco. I strongly encouraged him, after giving him some recommendations about his diet and the elimination crises that would probably occur.

So, he left, and I had no news from him for 4 years. What had become of him? That was a question I often asked myself. When, in 1994, at the Natural Medicine Geneva's Fair, a tall smiling bearded man walked to me saying: ***"Finally, I knew I would find you here!"***

Although he had lost a lot of weight, I instantly recognized him. His complexion and eyes were luminous, and he was wearing a bright smile.

"As you told me, I ate sprouts, fruits, and salads, and it was wonderful. And moreover, it was cheap. As you said, I had several bronchitis, that I treated by purging myself as you explained me. Each time I was surprised to feel better after the crisis. And this is not all, that is why I wanted to see you, my last tests showed no more viral load."

"I don't have HIV anymore, do you realize?"

Did I realize? Oh, so well! Do I have to mention, that, like for any other illness, we can recover from AIDS. If ever, like this man, we have a strong enough constitution and kept enough of instinct to understand and modify our mistakes. I will add that, being fragilized anyway, like all the patients of that kind, he will have to maintain this diet for his whole life.

One more time, can't we be amazed by the spectacular simplicity of life intelligence?

To be as clear as possible, I would like you to read this extract of "La Mafia Médicale"(*"The Medical Mafia"*), a French book written by Dr Ghislaine Lanctôt about the "origins of the HIV".

The HIV was officially "discovered" in 1983. Some persons looked carefully at this question and found out some surprising discovery that led them to conclude that it was a lab's creation instead of an already existing virus' discovery.

In 1985, Robert Stecker, a gastroenterologist and pharmacology doctor, concluded that the AIDS had been purposely created, either deliberately or by accident, while testing some new vaccine against hepatitis B for homosexuals.

He is convinced that African's continent was also contaminated, at the time of vaccination against smallpox, to study, on behalf of the WHO, the effects of some bacteria and viruses.

He explains that HIV cannot be natural, so different from other viruses, and that it would be a cloning of animals' viruses which, inoculated to human beings, built a new disease.

In 1992, Dr Eva Lee Snead, a holistic doctor and researcher, established the similarity of the clinical syndromes between HIV and SV40 of African green monkeys', that was found in some subjects.

"The only possibility for a human being to contract the monkey's SV40, is through eating its flesh or by being inoculated with a vaccine. This same SV40 was also found in the Sabine vaccine against poliomyelitis and commonly called "monkey soup" by scientists, with which millions of children were vaccinated for many years.

Yet, we observed that the SV40 caused birth defect, leukemias, cancers, and a serious immune depression equal to that of AIDS.

Dr Snead showed a relation between leukemia, SV40, and AIDS. For her, AIDS is a sort of leukemia. She also revealed the impact of vaccination in the emergence of AIDS and in the increase of leukemias and cancers.

Some groups of homosexuals having been secretly and prematurely vaccinated against hepatitis B, they probably developed this disease, that was finally attributed to them.

(...)

***1952** Closed meeting in Ottawa of American, English, and Canadian researchers about retroviruses*

***1959** The WHO reports the dangers of vaccines made with monkeys' biological material*

***1960** The WHO alerts on the presence of unexpected and unwanted viruses in vaccines*

***1960** The SV40 virus is identified in African green monkey's cells cultures and it appears that SV40 was present in most of the anti-polio with live viruses' vaccine, produced before this date.*

***1961** Vaccination with live viruses starts.*

***1963** A "tumor-producing" (likely to create tumors) virus coming from monkeys is signaled*

***1963** A report points out a raise of leukemias in the states where the anti-polio SV40 was administered.*

***1963** A research program starts, managed by the CIA and the US Army of Fort Detrick, Maryland, in coordination with the National Cancer Institute of Bethesda, near the capital Washington.*

***1964** SV40 virus is discovered in children's blood after they received the Sabin polio vaccine.*

***1964** Vaccines with live viruses seem to cause malignant diseases.*

These affections grow in the population:

1. Immune system deficiencies

2. Congenital defects

3. Leukemias

4. Malignant illnesses appear in young children

***1968** American virologists settle their sophisticated material in Zaïre*

***1969** President Nixon announces his intention to suspend biological weapons production and to destroy the existing stocks*

***1969** Research against cancer is greatly promoted. Retroviruses are scrutinized as it is known that they can cause cancers in animals, why not in human beings? These retroviruses are grown inside human cells. We do know now how to create a cancer!*

***1970** The WHO and the NIH (National Institute of Health) decide to inject viruses and bacteria to children during a vaccination campaign, to carry out a study.*

***1971** It is demonstrated that the SV40 causes cancer in mice.*

***1972** The WHO transforms the 1970's study into a study on the viruses that provoke a weakening of the immune system.*

1973 *Paul Berg and other famous names of Biochemistry disclose the general principles of a new science. The Genetic engineering is born.*

1973 *Discovery of a new retrovirus, the BIV* (bovine immunodeficiency virus)

1974 *The hereditary transmission of a foreign gene is now mastered.*

1975 *Robert Gallo, an American researcher, discovers the HTLV III and declares that this virus causes leukemia in certain groups of population.*

1977 *First cases of Immune acquired deficiency in an African female Doctor, followed by a number of cases in Haiti, drug addicts and hemophiliacs.*

1978 *The vaccination against hepatitis B starts in the New York homosexual community*

1980 *The vaccination against hepatitis B starts in five other cities in the USA*

1980 *Numerous cases of immune deficiency appear out of the pre-existing frame*

1981 *The AIDS epidemics officially starts*

1983 *Official discovery of a retrovirus said to be responsible of AIDS. Its name is the same as the illness "Human Immunedeficiency Virus" HIV*

***1992** After ten years of research, the most costly and intense ever done on a same disease, we realize how little we know about AIDS*

The most worrying aspect of this observation is the possibility that our ignorance is due to the immense faith that we put in the HIV theory, and the insufficient attention that we paid to its critics.

On top of that, each year, more people claim that HIV alone cannot cause AIDS and consequently, controlling AIDS, focusing on vaccines, drugs or even public policies are not sufficient." Something else has to be done.

Signed by: Robert Root-Bernstein, Professor of physiology at the University of Michigan, also biochemist and immunologist.

Fortunately, some doctors start to challenge these questions. Let us hope that they will be more and more; until one day, we understand that viruses or retroviruses can only live and develop in an environment that provides the food they need to grow.

After 40 years of intense fight and billions of Dollars spent in research, we must admit that, not only has the death rate of AIDS not diminished, but on the contrary it has raised! Failure? For who, if not the patients to whom we can chose to belong or not!

Yes, we can choose!

On condition of course, and this is the purpose of this book, to know that we are able to choose according to **"THE COMMON SENSE"**, the sense of life, of all its beneficence. Using our intuition, we know that it exists. But, if we are deficient, poisoned, conditioned, we totally ignore it.

In its great simplicity and immense splendor, Life gave us everything to be happy and make our journey on earth, a true paradise.

Of course, if we start by respecting the 4 basic laws of our functioning, and there are:

Breathing, Eating, Sleeping, and Eliminating.

Allowing us, you cannot ignore it anymore, to connect to the life frequencies, whose state of consciousness, ideas and feelings will guide us, for our best and the good of all, if they are respected. And if not, our lives will be a true hell.

Hence the interest to start from the beginning, which is to take the best care of our body. This amazing laboratory that allows us to love, think and act. To simply live!

Because, if the truth is that we can love with our soul and think with our mind, and if these two functions were always considered superior. It is also true, and even undisputable, that in order to love as well as we think, we need our body and its precious cells.

This also means, that even if psychological and personal development techniques of all kinds are so precious in times of trouble; we have to keep in mind that they will never, never ever, be able to give oxygen or food to our cells, nor clean the liquids in which they bathe.

And, considering these two elements that I find essential, all our behaviors will lead us to a healthy, happy, and successful life, if they are respected; or to a painful life whatsoever if they are not.

This is why all the religions of the world suggested that their believers practice fasting and abstinence, in order to raise their spiritual level, which is the level of a higher connection reached by fasting.

These precious cells which, besides maintaining our body healthy and our link with the universal intelligence; seem to perfectly keep the books of our feelings, thoughts, and acts. So that when we reach the end of the journey, they can memorize them in our subtle bodies like soul and spirit.

Or, to be more up to date, keep them in our hard drive, so that for our next journey, more precisely our next incarnation, we find them in our luggage called genetics or subconscious.

Accepting this hypothesis could explain life a different way, and also the reason why, perhaps, we were born so different.

To accept this hypothesis
might explain the inexplicable
and justify the unjustifiable!

That doesn't prevent us from wondering "Who? What?", backstage, is pulling the strings of this extraordinary enterprise that allows us to live.

Breathing

Starting from the beginning, which is, as we have seen in the first pages of this book, to breathe widely, deeply, and consciously as often as possible. And, as we are born and leave this world with a sigh, we have to also admit the importance of breathing, without which we cannot live longer than 3 minutes.

Except for the trained yogis or the pearl divers in the Fiji Islands, who practice extensively and can live up to 6 minutes or more without breathing.

The role of breathing is to bring oxygen to the blood, which turns bright red. Oxygenated blood flows through the aorta to our various arteries, which divide into arterioles and then capillaries, to nourish even the smallest cells in our body. Then the venous circulation carries the blood, loaded with carbon dioxide or CO_2, to the lungs through the pulmonary artery. The blood is freed of CO_2, re enriched with oxygen, and the cycle begins again.

According to its breathing capacities, which can vary from 10 to 30 cubic meters *(2642 to 7925 US gallons)* a day, our blood oxygenation had a particular impact on our cells' life, and consequently, on all our behavior.

The air contains nearly 20% oxygen and 70% nitrogen. It also contains a certain number of other gas like carbon dioxide (a mixture of carbon and oxygen), hydrogen, and noble gas (neon, krypton, helium, xenon, argon), traces of nitrous and nitric acid, ammoniac, water steam and also aromas from plants, not forgetting the Hindu Prana that we call ***"biotons"*** in naturopathy, largely and beneficially used also in qi gong or tai chi chuan practice.

Generating life, "biotons" maintain the "vital force", also called "vitality", residing in our endocrine glands and nervous system.

Such is the natural air that we should breathe, according to Pierre Valentin Marchesseau, the founder of the French Naturopathic School.

Unfortunately, the air of urban and industrial areas, contains a large quantity of carbon dioxide (CO_2), some formic acid, chlorine, sulfur compounds, burnt soot and tar and many other poisons, in higher levels than normal.

We say that it is polluted.

It also contains all the dust that we see in a ray of sun, the fluff, hair, mold, spores, and all sorts of staphylococcus, streptococcus, and bacillus. In downtown Paris, we can find up to 1 000 bacteria per cubic meter of air, at 8 am on Place de l'Étoile, and almost 100 000 at 6 pm. Needless to say that this air is totally inadequate for human life.

In the countryside as well as on the open sea or in the mountain, above 2 000 meters or around 6 500 feet, the rate of germs is almost null where it is aseptic. Concentrated oxygen can turn into ozone (1 mg for 100 cubic meter of air), which ratio raises in the countryside, forests, mountains' heights, near springs and cascades, in the morning, at dawn, when the birds sing, or after storm rains. Etc.

The pollution peaks prevent certain beneficial radiations from reaching us, they hold back the toxic gas on the surface of the earth and disorganize the climate.

More than any other organ, the brain is a great consumer of oxygen.

This is why, intellectuals more than others, need to have a respiratory physical practice. Like any of us should also do, by breathing more consciously, more profoundly, more largely and more often as possible.

The best would be, of course, to breathe in a pure and sunny air or in a perfumed environment rich in negative ions.

Do not mix up the negative ions with the positive ions, which are atoms or molecules that lost their peripheric electrons. But, urban life, concrete buildings, being away from the forest, losing contact with the ground, induced current, crowds' meetings, and dead, chemical, cooked food, have a tendency to make humans electrically positive, which weakens them when they lose their "negative ions".

Fortunately, we can recharge with special electric currents, seat bath friction, walking barefoot on the ground or in the dew, eating raw vegetable, or with aromas that seem to be the surest way for electrons transfer. Reasons why, in the Winter season, it is necessary to breathe in a room bathed in aerosols with natural and aromatic essential oils.

This air improves our health and enhances the healing of sick people.

However, let us keep in mind that a respiratory insufficiency does not allow our body to get enough oxygen, and breathing polluted air does not allow the rejection of carbon dioxide.

In other words, both do not let the oxidation-reduction that is necessary for the growth and lifespan of living creatures. Thus, provoking a slow asphyxia, which has a pernicious incidence on our health.

This being said, should we breathe through the nose or through the mouth?

The inspire is normally done through widely open nostrils, mouth closed. This is the rule during the idle rest or with slow and non-violent movements that do not require an intense pulmonary activity. It is discussed by all those who are in charge of health (physiotherapists, gym yoga dance Kung-Fu teachers). For some, it must be done noisily, through a slightly open mouth (body builders, athletes), and for others, it should be done exclusively through the nose (yogis).

In reality, they are all wrong... and also right.

Because the mouth is not only a pre-digestive organ, it is also a phonatory organ. Speaking, singing, coughing are expiratory actions, and since expiring through the nose only allows a small quantity of air, we instinctively use our mouth, through which 6 to 10 times the volume of the nose can be liberated.

However, this emergency measure, as it dries, cools down and drains the nasal mucous membrane, by removing the humid warmth, should only be used for important breathlessness conditions.

This is why, breathing through the nose, which is especially designed for this function, is recommended.

The interior of the nose is covered with a thick mucous membrane, with hair, blood vessels, glands, and nerves, which are also filters, disinfectants, heaters, and humidifiers of the air that we breathe. The nose is also equipped with a subtle touch-sensitive keypad related to all the trigger points of the body, using the sympathetic system on which the air, not only acts as stimulant and vitalizer, but also as an alarm, using the sense of smell.

Many reasons to easily see, through the multiple functions of nasal breathing, the inconvenience of mouth breathing.

The olfactory brain (brain of the nose) does not only serve for smelling odors, but also to behave carefully, with discernment, for the sake of our species.

This is why, to cauterize, modify or remove some parts of the nose may diminish or abolish some protection instincts.

The olfactory brain is one of the keys of intuition and premonition. Probably the origins of expression "to have a nose for something".

The nasal permeability plays a very important role in children's growth and health. This explains why the children who breathe through the mouth (those who have lots of more or less dry viscosities in the nose or respiratory tract), have a slower brain development.

A deep and complete breathing soothes and puts the psyche at rest and dreamful.

It recharges the nervous batteries.

Reasons why, although it is more and more difficult to breath in large cities where the air is polluted, and because sedentary lifestyle permanently asphyxiates us, **we will try to practice some respiratory exercises every day. If possible, we will do it in a pure-air environment, or in an ionized room, using essential oils which all are revitalizing, bactericides, purifying, enhancing elimination, and ionizing.**

We know all kind of breathing methods. But we will remain careful about some specific techniques, highly sophisticated, which could, instead of enlightening us, lead to a disaster. Not because they are wrong, but because the energy produced by breathing, just like the one made by live food and dietary supplements, can cause psychological elimination crises. They can be beneficial if they are controlled but may have serious consequences if not.

This is thus necessary not to use these high-level methods if they are not correctly prepared and coached.

Until now, we believed that food was as necessary to our cells, as oxygen. Today, following the methods of "prânism", and "respirianism", oxygen could be more important than food, because, according to highly technical breathing techniques, **the persons who practice could avoid eating and drinking.**

Even if this is possible, let us start by simply breathing, each one at our own pace, as often and widely as possible.

Especially when we feel overwhelmed by low, dark ideas, sometimes painful, distressful, and destructive, or if, for any reason, our heart, or another part of our body aches. **We will soon realize that, by practicing some good breathing, within in a short time, pain will end.**

The oxygen brought by breathing will allow our cells to reach a higher frequency, our state of consciousness will raise. Through a good oxygenation by breathing well, we will access to *"noble and high feelings will arise, with clear, constructive ideas and the energy to fulfill them"*.

We all know that, when a problem is on his way to be solved, we can "*finally breathe*".

This is the main and so important reason for understanding the importance of breathing. We should breathe as often as possible, deeply, widely, and consciously, during the day.

Starting as we wake up, with a nice breathing session and, when possible, continued outside, to thank life and all the gifts she offers, as we will see later.

This will have the most positive incidence on our day!

Food classification

According to Dr Bordeaux Szekely's work, whom I consider as the safest reference speaking about nutrition, we will classify nutrients in four categories, which have nothing to see with the standard classification based on proteins, lipids, carbohydrates, and calories. But upon their ability to produce life, to sustain it, or to slow and destroy it.

Nutrients that he called:

- **Biogenics**, when they produce life energy or vitality.
- **Bioactives,** when they sustain it
- **Biostatics,** when they put it down
- **Biocides**, when they destroy it

Honor to whom honor is due, let us start with the "biogenic" food (which in ancient Greek means, "that bring life").

Biogenic nutrients are only those offered by nature the way they are produced. The original ones that we can consume without any transformation. Besides natural and pure water, they are constituted of fruits, vegetables, all raw and without treatment, and eaten right after they were gathered. Also, young shoots and sprouted seeds, which, again according to Dr Szekely are of the highest energetic value.

Out of his research, he found that sprouted seeds were the Essene people food, who were said to be healthy, have a joy of life and spirituality beyond compare. Still according to him, young shoots and sprouted seeds can synthesize biological compounds that perpetrate higher functions, like the destruction of toxins produced by improper food. They reinforce the transport of oxygen in blood and intra cellular circulation, they stimulate the biological resistance and sustain the natural process of self-healing that Pliny the Elder called *"vix medicatrix naturae" (the regenerative power of nature).*

With these first-class nutrients, we avoid the destruction of enzymes and also the deterioration of certain amino acids and proteins when they are cooked, which produces – we know it – toxic substances. We also prevent the destruction of vitamins through conditioning or artificial substances addition and the suppression of natural nutritional substances.

Moreover, these nutrients have the great advantage to be digested without producing leukocytosis, which is a kind of digestive leukemia, caused by a raise in the number of blood lymphocytes. It always arises after what we call "a great dinner" made of anti-specific and cooked food (after-meal sleep).

With this exceptional food, the lymphocytes remain intact and available for our immune system.

Sprouted seeds are also among the cheapest foods.

A 1.10 lbs. of seeds produces more than 8.8 lbs. of sprouted seeds. One tablespoon of alfalfa gives 0.55 lbs. Who could do better? They only require a few minutes of your attention each morning and evening, for every two- or three-days harvest.

Their fast gathering brings them from the pot to the plate in a few minutes. They do not require any specific equipment but one or two sprouters. Anyone can grow seeds. Neither age nor physical condition are limiting factors. They are the cheapest means to bring everyone biogenic food, rich in minerals, enzymes, vitamins, and proteins.

Some experimental facts.

In 0.1 lbs. of sprouted oats there are 15mg (300 IU) of vitamin C, that is more than in the same quantity contained in a melon, black current or blueberry.

After 72 hours of germination, soya beans raise their vitamin C concentration by 553%.

After a few days of germination, wheat raises its vitamin C concentration by 600%.

Oats' sprouted seeds raise their vitamin B concentration by 1300%. When the green shoots appear from the seed, the raise reaches 2000%.

Dr Burkholder also observed the following raises: pyridoxin (vit. B6) 500 %, pantothenic acid 200 %, folic acid 600 %, biotin 50 %, inositol 100 %, nicotinic acid 500 %.

Dr Jr. Pottinger in California declares that sprouted legumes and sprouted seeds contain first quality proteins. The germination techniques are extremely simple, and you also find them with a selection of recipes in "Graines germées" by Marcel Monnier or "Manger soleil" at Editions Soleil (NDA: *and in English "Sprouts the miracle food" by Steve Meyerowitz – The sproutman – www.Sproutman.com).*

This simple and natural food develops our own healing capacities and thanks to the self-regeneration strength that it passes to our body, it can produce efficient antibodies against infections, bone-fracture repairing or wounds healing. This food is not only rich and tasty, but it is also the most economical live food you can eat.

This is why, with fruits and raw vegetables, shoots and sprouted seeds really are the "super food" of our body. They are highly digestible and bring a maximum of nutritional and energetic nutrients, that leave few toxins.

Energy + Clean Cells = Health

Although these foods possess all the desired qualities, we eat more easily **what Szekely calls "bioactive" food.**

Like the treated fruits and vegetables that we currently find, and eat long after they were collected, sometimes sterilized, pasteurized and frozen. They are also fermented vegetables or algaes, seafood - not to be mistaken with crustacean - honey, yeasts, bottled mineral water or herbal teas. Although they lost a part of their energy, these nutrients still remain quite favorable for our health.

Then, we have the "biostatic" foods, that I call tolerant

Like potatoes, tubers cooked in water or in the oven, chestnuts, wholegrains, pasta, pastries, and wholegrain bread. Slightly cooked eggs, curd, yoghurt, fresh or blue cheese, wild fish, organic poultry, veggie terrine, cooked mushrooms, brown sugar, fructose, maple syrup, and all these whole and natural nutrients that are particularly recommended in a 20th century vegetarian diet.

On the same subject, let me give you the definition of the word "vegetarian", that I found in a conventional cookbook.

Unlike what we could expect, vegetarian does not come from vegetable but from the Latin word "vegetus" which means "in a good health". The vegetarian diet would then be the ideal diet to be healthy. Excluding all cadaveric animal products, this diet offers a great variety. It brings calories as well as nitrogen, and when they contain sugar or oil, their waste is mostly made of cellulose which is useful for a good intestine functioning, carbon dioxide and steam, which are harmless, and also very few uric acid if they are nitrogen-based.

We will continue by saying that vegetables are also a precious source of vitamins that produce serious troubles when they lack, like deficiency diseases. Another advantage is that they alter slower than animal-issued food. The residues of this alteration are less dangerous than the ptomaine that comes from animal tissues. We will finally conclude by saying that vegetables are less expensive than a nutrition-equivalent piece of meat.

Telling you how this article surprised me is not necessary.

Except for fish that they catch and eat fresh, we could say that this diet is close to the Cretan diet, famous for the good health of the island's inhabitants, even if it still not perfect.

Szekely called "biocide" the food that, without any remorse, I qualify as murderous.

Because, just like any other weapon, they finally make us sick and kill us. This food belongs to the rich, civilized, and industrialized countries. It is made of red meat, wild game, charcuteries, crustaceans like lobsters, crayfish, and shrimps, which are sea scavengers, and all wines and other alcohols that go with them.

It is also made up of the refined and cooked cereals and their derivatives, like white bread, white rice, pasta, pizza and all the "viennoiseries", hamburgers, fries, and all fried food. Then we have poultry, eggs and farmed fish, hydrogenated oils and margarines, butter, cream, cheese, and dairy products, as well as industrialized food. And let us not forget the refined sugar and all its derivatives that we find in pastries, jams, treats, chocolate, ice creams... Sodas, coffees, teas, wines and alcohols, are at the origin of most of humanity's disasters. Also, with preservatives, synthetic, ionized and genetically modified products.

These are clearly the products that the food industry commonly sells and that we should replace with tolerance foods, before getting used to eat more and more natural and live food, that nature, so generously provides, when we most need it and the way it decided for us.

That is the freshest and rawest possible, **hoping to live a forever happy and long life.**

How to shift to a live diet

Considering that our current diet is so different from the original one, it may happen that even if you want to find it, you wonder how and by what to start with.

No matter how, what is important is to start with what you enjoy the most, and do like the mountain climber who, even if he does not walk straight to the peak, never loses it from sight.

That is to say, to accept our weaknesses, without forgetting that our body was crafted to work with the food provided by nature and the way it was planned. This will encourage you to progress towards a more and more live food and discover or re-discover the wellbeing automatically associated with it.

Except of course, if you suffer from real health conditions, in which case you will have to look for an experienced therapist.

But if not, and if you are not ready to radically change your diet, the best would be to start with your breakfast. Instead of having coffee, tea, or chocolate, which are not foods but stimulants, you will start with a large glass of water, warm or cold. If you prefer it hot, you can pour in 4 drops of cinnamon essential oil, one of clove, a drop of honey with lemon juice, which make a tonic and pleasant drink. Or a hot drink with ginger, lemon, and honey in water, to start the day. If you prefer cold water, you can add a vial of nettle juice, horsetail, some ginseng, sea water plasma (Quinton water), according to your needs.

I imagine you understand that it is not normal to kickstart a day with a stimulant like coffee or tea, right after a whole night of sleep.

Considering that this is such a habit, you may not want in the first place, to change it right away.

In this case please, at least, have your tea or coffee after enjoying your favorite fruits that you will eat as it is or blended in a smoothie or puree. Go for recipes at www.santenaturopathie.com

How many fruits can I eat?

Knowing that the fruits you like the most are the ones that your body needs, eat all the fruits you like and enjoy them.

Your body will tell you when it has got enough.

It will not be so with cooked and processed food, which we can drink or eat much over our real needs. For the simple reason that, with this food, our cells function the wrong way and start enjoying, asking, and demanding the products that make the poison in which they are immersed.

This means that, if we like grape, we can eat it as long as we enjoy it, whereas if we like wine, which is made of processed grape, the risk is to drink more than reasonable, or even more. But let us go back to our breakfast.

Do you like oranges, kiwis, grapefruits, lemons and all these acidic fruits? Go ahead, if you like them, that means your body needs their substances and will be happy to use them and de-acidify your blood.

Yes, these fruits called acidic are an excellent solvent to destroy uric acid.

So, trust your body, and give it they fruit that it likes.

If you like them too, you can also take some dates, figs, or dry and sweet fruits, which you eat plain or dipped into in a small amount of water the day before. Their sugar, which has nothing to do with industrial sugar, is your best source of energy.

Do you prefer apples, pears, or bananas?

You can eat them on their own, but also with all kind of nuts: hazelnuts, almonds... and some sweet dried fruits like dates or figs, if you like them.

Do you prefer cherries, apricots, peaches, and nectarines?

These fruits are sufficient on their own, and perfectly correspond to our needs, according to the season when they grow.

When the weather is really cold, you might prefer a hot breakfast?

That is alright! For one serving, put 6 to 8 dates or 2 to 3 big medjool dates and remove their pits, in a blender, add a handful of cashew, hazelnuts, walnuts or almonds, and mix it all, while boiling some water that you will gently add to the mixture. Then enjoy your meal!

But I will be starving to death, eating only fruits!

I am laughing! Fruits are much more energetic and nutritional than butter and jam toasts you usually have, and much easier to digest, with the little residue that they leave for elimination. They will bring you a considerable energy.

But I will get fat eating fruits!

Of course not! I can assure you that the best weight loss I had seen, were when people eat fruits, and even bananas. Please, do not mix up the idea of live and energetic fruits, with dead, inert, and poisonous sugar of industrial carbohydrates.

Yes, but since I had a gastroenteritis, my doctor recommends avoiding them!

Of course, and he had two good reasons for that. The first one is, that in College, he did not learn that a gastroenteritis is the manifestation of a wrong diet, and that one should rather help the body to get rid of its waste than stop the gastroenteritis.

The second one is, that fresh fruits and raw vegetables are live food. Which means active substances which, instead of plugging your intestines, eating your usual dead food, helps the elimination process.

This explains the bloating, spasms and colic, all elimination's signs that happen for your best. This colic will cease when its work is done. Sometimes, it can last several weeks or more.

Following that, you will be able to eat as many fruits and raw vegetables as you wish without any trouble.

If you are in this case, I recommend not to start your meal with raw vegetables, as you will do later, but with lacto-fermented vegetables to ease this cleansing and surprisingly renew your microbiota.

Anyway, you should know that "*fruits are Lords that don't like promiscuity*". So, instead of eating them for dessert, like you have been doing until now, you should try entire fruit meals.

When?

Each time you feel like it. For breakfast, lunch, it is quite easy if you work outside, or for dinner if you have sleeping problems.

Can I combine them?

Of course, just observe the great apes who have a similar digestive system as us, human being. And see that they eat fruits, soft leaves, or roots as they find them. I am sorry to compare us to animals, but considering we have the same digestive tract, it means that we should eat the same food.

Same engine, same fuel, isn't it? *Which are the best fruits*?

There are no best fruits. But there are some fruits best for you. As you know it now, the best fruits for you, are the ones you prefer.

Remember that your food's instinct best works facing natural and raw plants and is the best laboratory that you could have. So, if you like apples, eat them, and if you prefer bananas or kiwis eat them as long as you like them. Because, as soon as your body will not need it, you won't enjoy them anymore.

It is so amazing to realize that each fruit, each vegetable, or each plant is a biochemical compound that our taste will detect, in order to satisfy our physiological needs.

Personally, the more I understand the rules of life, the more I see that everything was made for our happiness, and that we must be really mentally disoriented, to be sick, to suffer and be as unhappy as we are.

Each one of us, being so particular, the fruits and vegetables we love may not please or be suitable for someone else. So, let us not impose our taste to anyone.

Another thing, if eating raw fruit is easy, how should we eat vegetables?

As raw as possible of course. The first habit that we should take, is to start our meal with crudités that we can season to our taste with all sorts of aromatic herbs like parsley, chives, chervil, tarragon, basil, marjoram, mint, coriander... Which not only will please our mouth, but also help our digestion while preventing guts putrefactions.

Yes, but fresh aromatic plants are expensive!

This is true. But in reality, they are much less expensive that cheese and meat, chocolate, alcohol, and tobacco, which, not only don't contribute to our health but rather deteriorate it.

And you could grow them in your garden, on your balcony, or even in a large tray behind a window. Which will not only spread their lovely perfume, but also be ready to collect whenever you need them.

And yet, how should we season those crudites?

With first cold pressed oil, of course, from peanut, sunflower, sesame, olive, walnut, safflower... Or with avocado, walnuts, black olives... (green olives having most of the time their bitterness chemically removed).

Vegetable fat is essential for the functioning of our brain cells. You will also add some sea salt of course, or some mixed salt and herbs, a squeeze of lemon juice or small pieces of orange or grapefruit to deliciously refine your salad. Do not forget garlic, the lord of crystalloids types, and finely diced onion for the colloidal types.

Yes, but I will smell garlic and onion!

This is true, but only until your digestive secretions are unable to assimilate these precious condiments. The first thing to do, is not to avoid them, but rather dose them and stop ruining your digestive secretions with vinegar, alcohol or other "supposed foods". Considering that you can take one or two drops of peppermint essential oil, or another one that you like, to neutralize their smell.

Yes, but salads and raw vegetables make me bloat and give me colitis

It is clear, because at the beginning of your dietary transition, they take the opportunity to cleanse your dirt and muck, left by your cooked food. Not being able to eliminate it, your body someway upholstered your gut pipes with it.

This is the cause of the bloating and gas, which tear off this dirt that goes in your feces. This condition that you will try to stop, by eating cooked and dead food, which only increases this padding, and prevents your intestine to recover their beneficial function, is called colitis.

In this case, drinking a fresh glass of vegetable juice to replace the raw crudites, or even some lacto-fermented juice, will help you restore your microbiota.

And for the best, you will continue your meal with lacto-fermented vegetables like raw sauerkraut and any other lacto-fermented veggies, so easy to prepare if you follow recipes founded on the Web.

If you are not ready yet for a total dietary change, you could continue by taking just decruited vegetables, the way the Asians cook them, or have them steamed, cooked in the oven or braised, in the beginning.

For all the persons in pain, vegetable juices are the best remineralizing foods they can offer to their body. For the good reason that vegetables are full of minerals, and since we do not eat enough raw vegetables, the daily intake of one or two veggie juices on top of your salads, will double the mineral sypply.

This shows the interest of vegetable juice, a concentrate of minerals. But for fruits, we will avoid juice, and eat them entirely, with the pulp.

It doesn't mean that you cannot add some apple or orange to soften your veggie juices. You can also put some aromatic plants, ginger, curcuma, or green stinging nettle if you have some nearby.

Nettle are the antidote to coffee...

They are the best anti-depressant plant ever and there are cheap!

So, enjoy them!

Should we eat only organic fruits and vegetables?

That would be the best of course. Firstly, you should know where to buy them, because even if they are widely distributed, you may not find them in some places. Since growing them is more time consuming, they are more expensive, and their price might be a problem. At least until you have compared them with the chemically treated vegetables and fruits that you usually buy but will soon refuse.

Their price is not such an obstacle, if you consider that eating them raw requires smaller quantities than when they are cooked. On my opinion, and it may not be yours, even chemically treated, raw veggies and fruits are better than cooked and dead food like bread, rice, pasta, meat, coffee, wine, and cheese, even if they are organic....

What vegetables can we eat raw?

Almost all, except perhaps potatoes, although its juice is excellent against stomach acidity and ulcer. Eggplants maybe, with which, coming back from Greece, I said to myself that I should try a raw moussaka, and I can tell you, it was delicious.

It is the asparagus season. But we cannot eat them raw, can we?

Do not be mistaken, whether white or green, their tender stem is absolutely delicious with lemon juice, olive oil and chives seasoning. Instead of eating 1.1 to 1.3 lbs (500 to 600 grams). when cooked, you will enjoy five or six raw stems and save money. And like Mediterranean do, you can also eat raw artichokes.

But you may be tired of eating raw food every day?

Are you tired of eating potatoes, rice, pasta, and hamburgers each day, which, even if you think that you love them, become annoying and insipid? And even if you do not totally enjoy them at the beginning, you will, one day, enjoy raw veggies.

Personally, I never have enough meals in the season, to enjoy the great variety of fruits, vegetables, and greens that Nature offers us. And this is without mentioning sprouts which, just on their own, are a whole universe of tastes, shapes, and colors, as well as algae and lacto-fermented vegetables.

I never heard of that, what is it?

As we briefly mentioned, lacto-fermented vegetables are excellent means to repair the microbiota, which is always deficient in all constipated, anxious persons, and for those who suffer from respiratory illnesses. You should read Dr Kull's book about juices and lacto-fermented vegetables. He healed many degenerative sick persons with them. The most common vegetables used for lacto-fermentation are cabbages with which one makes sauerkraut, carrots, cucumbers, black radish, red beet, kohlrabi and are largely used in Poland and in the north of Russia when they lack of fresh vegetables during the long winters.

Talking about algae, they contain about 95 trace elements among the 100 listed. Japan or Korea as well as many coastal countries largely consume them. They are generally cooked, but of course, are better when eaten raw. And since we are talking about the sea, let us have a look at the food of the sea or seafood, like oysters, mussels, urchins, the delicious purple ones. But forget, if possible, bread, butter and wine and rather season them with a lemon squeeze.

Seafood is so rich in trace elements, that they can help the detox process, provoking some diarrhea or vomiting, to expel our stored residues. Far from being an intoxication, they cause a beneficial cleansing and elimination crisis.

But do not mix up with crustaceans, like shrimps, lobsters, and crawfish, which are sea scavengers that need to be cooked and are extremely acidifying.

Just a word about sprouts that were the food of the Essene among whom it is said that Jesus grew up.

Sprouts are so exceptional that they could just by themselves end alcoholism, violence, drug addiction and world starvation. And moreover, they are really cheap and so easy to grow, even children can do it.

This brings us back to this so "tiny error", that cooking food is.

Heating was the start of all our misery. We will never end wars and illnesses fighting against them, but by repairing this error at the origin of all our sufferings, pains, wars and illnesses.

Starting with the least to be done: "treat our body as well as we treat our car".

Which means, give it the right fuel that its founder, called the Creator, designed for its best functioning, and the way it should be done, raw and vegetal. And of course, with the necessary maintenance and draining that go well.

This one little thing could change our entire life. By connecting ourselves to the Universal Intelligence, we will constantly be guided and informed. In order to make of our lives and that of the earth, this paradise of joy, wellbeing, love, and creativity that we all seek and for which life gave us everything.

Let us tell each other!

Dietary supplements

"The remedy is always next to the illness".

Considering our usual diet which not only intoxicated us, but also deprived us, the idea of dietary supplements emerged in the 1930's in order to help us to compensate the energetic and nutritional loss of a more and more anti specific, processed and deficient food.

It was well accepted by researchers like Shute, Kaufmann, Hoffer, Williams and Linus Pauling, Peace Noble Prize winner in 1954, who discovered that a biochemical and cellular imbalance always and since long, precedes a clinically discovered illness.

Linus Pauling, called orthomolecular medicine, the therapeutic use of food supplements. "Ortho" means according to the best individual needs, brought by essential nutrients which are:

- **Vitamins,**
- **Minerals and trace elements,**
- **Fatty acids and amino acids...**

That food should bring to our body, if only we eat live, natural, and specific. New discoveries were made later by Henri Laborit, Carl Pfeiffer, Lesser, Roy Walford, Atkins, Nieper, and many others like Dr Kousmine and P.V. Marchesseau, who glimpsed at the important role played by dietary supplements in our civilized diet. This is why I find highly interesting to use dietary supplements.

My main difficulty was to find the right diet supplements, and the best amount for each person, in order to rebalance them nutrients levels.

Because despite their indications, it rapidly appeared that some supplements that suited a person might not correspond to another one having the same illness. Moreover, as they are costly, I had to council them as wisely as possible.

My questions were: who needed exactly what, in which amount, when and how long.

I therefore looked for a device to give me theses indications, but not finding it, I relied on this Universe Intelligence that leads us. Two years passed, before I went to visit a laboratory producing essential oils and herbal remedies. A lab' created by an exceptional pharmacist. I did say exceptional, because in a time where chemical drugs were considered a cure-all, he refused to sell them.

"Nature gave us herbs with which we make essential oils, and with this, I can do everything. I will never sell this crap!" he said. Buses full of tuberculosis patients came to see him. Due to his success, he was sued 13 times by the French pharmacist's association, his colleagues. He lost 12 trials and won the 13th, after what he created his own company called DIETAROMA. Dazzled by this clear and bright 84 years old person when I met him. I noticed he had a little something turning in is fingers, so I asked him what it was.

"*I will never give this little thing for anything in the world*", he answered me very seriously. "*With it, I can even control the errors of my team.*"

I started to imagine that it was perhaps the machine I had been looking for, and without waiting any longer I asked him if I could learn how to use it. He put it into my hands and said that there was no doubt.

Why and how did I see it,
I do not know.

Later, following this pretended "chance" that knows things well, I went to a conference on radiesthesia dowsing given by a Professor at the College de France.

Immediately after this conference that stunned me, I enrolled in his class and soon, felt to be led by some invisible guide and since then, each day I thank Heaven.

Still, as I am a colloidal type, it took me some time before I worked with it in my consultations. And since then, I have never stopped using it. Even if it was not always easy to step aside from this pendulum which I sometimes threw away, thinking that I was getting stupid. But the information it gave me was so true, that I soon put my ego aside. As this precious guidance allowed me to help my patients recover their health and well-being faster.

Thanks to it, I could recommend not only the herbs, essential oils, and dietary supplements that my clients needed the most, but also bath, exercises or other techniques adapted to their specific needs. Not forgetting the food that would be the best for them. Feeling guided that way, my life was radically transformed, and I went from a happy surprise to another.

Of one them was, that the many smokers that I treated for their health conditions, suddenly lost their addiction.

"*What did you put in my program*" asked one of them one day. "*I cannot put a cigarette in my mouth, and I feel so disgusted that I cannot smoke anymore*" said another.

To speak the truth, it was simply logical, because when a body receives nutrients and energy that it needs, it can live without stimulants. And since it is not excited anymore, it does not need these little doses of opiates (traces of opium) contained in tobacco, to soothe.

I also observed that overweight people and obese lost weight more rapidly

Radiesthesia not only helped me discover that the food intake reduction that I used to propose, was not enough. But that, most of the time, I had to start by providing my clients the vitality they needed to eliminate.

Which appeared to be a much easier and sustainable way to lose weight.

And what about the depressed persons who recovered their well-being surprisingly fast?

Besides the natural techniques taught by naturopathy, radiesthesia and orthomolecular nutrition became my best allies. I can now thank all the researchers who discovered, not the eternity elixir, which doesn't and will never exist, but the molecules that persons eating a poor nutritive food, need to recover this superior vitality and energy that we should all experience, if our food taken was as it should be.

As a conclusion, whatever precious they are, dietary supplements can only be used in addition with a more specific, natural, energetic, and live food. But they can help a lot during the dietary transition.

Fasting and mono diets

As we have seen several times, when our body has too much energy or need to face a shock, it instantly eliminates the poisoning residues stored in its deep layers.

And there starts this painful or annoying condition, and may be both, called illness. All our diseases, physical, mental, or psychological sufferings are in reality an alarm sent by our body, asking for help, in order to get rid of its residues and stop being poisoned.

Shall we understand and help it in this difficult but so life-saving task?

Or, influenced by fear, ignorance of the laws of life; shall we only try to mute our sufferings and illnesses, without wondering what created them and change our attitude?

In the first case, like all animals do each time they are wounded or "sick", we start with resting and fasting. This will allow our body to use all its energy to eliminate, instead of waste it in digesting or moving. And so, crisis after crisis, we will recover our health and well-being through the elimination process.

Let us remember that digestion in itself uses half of our energy, and that each elimination crisis requires a lot.

This explains the major interest of fasting and resting. While helping our body to use all its energy to eliminate our residues, we will allow us to heal from our diseases, and also to be linked to higher frequencies.

As we already know it, everything is vibration. According to the quality of our cells, of their functioning, the cleanliness of their liquids; we will be bound to higher frequencies if they work correctly, and to lower if they are weak, deficient, and intoxicated. This is why, most religions recommend to fast, in order to reach a higher spiritual level. Wasn't it after long illnesses which took them to fast, that most of the Saints accomplished miracles?

Whereas if they had been fed like kings, like all the meat eaters who drink alcohol, they would have gone to war or have a party. And instead of fasting and praying, they would have fought against their sufferings and illnesses. Without realizing that there is only one common cause: a diet that was against the laws of their physiology.

The same law that created the mad cow disease!

The cows' brain cells, like ours, did not accept foods unfit for their digestive tract. The paradox is that we seem to accept this fact for cows, but not for us.

How many more catastrophes shall we need before we understand that following the rules of our physiology to make of our lives a paradise, rather than hell, is simply enough?

How many wars, cries and pains shall we need, before we understand that, like parasites, microbes, and viruses of all kinds; our dark, destructive ideas and feelings cannot live without their food? And that the best way to remove them is not by fighting; but by depriving them of inappropriate food?

Yes, but to ask oneself the right questions, one has to be connected to the life intelligence.

And this is impossible for those whose cells are immersed in an acidic environment, which burns and destroys the minerals that they need to reach it. As well as for those whose cells are slowed down and paralyzed by their viscous magma.

Another reason for the necessity to bring our body the food planned by nature, and to cleanse the humors in which its precious cells are plunged.

In other words, the necessity to fast, like animals do naturally when they are sick or wounded, and that we should also practice if, like them, we still followed our instinct.

And they kept this instinct because they constantly ate what nature decided for their digestive system.

Whereas by eating hot and meaty foods since we discovered fire, we replaced our instinct by the intellect.

The intellect which, depending on the frequencies to which it is connected, can be negative and destructive, whereas the instinct is the result of high frequencies.

The high frequencies of life only want the best for its creatures.

Still considering that the intellect enables us to do lots of very interesting things, when our cells remain tuned with the frequencies of life. But if our cells are fragilized, deficient and poisoned, they can only connect to the frequencies they can reach. Which are as low and destructive as the cells are fragilized, deficient and poisoned.

Once this said, let us go back to fasting and diet that cleanse our body from its mucus. This matter in which the cells live, so that our little cells can connect with the frequencies that belong to the life intelligence, called by the religions, divine or spiritual.

Let us first have a look, at the liquid diet constituted of only water, herbal teas, or vegetable broth.

This diet is particularly recommended for the crystalloid types who need to drink as much liquid as possible, in order to drain the excess of uric acid in their blood and have less painful crises. Knowing that, like water needs soap to clean the dirty laundry, all the water we can absorb will not be able to dissolve and eliminate the acidic residues, without the saponifying and dissolving action of plants that we will discover later.

The second way to fast, is to not eat and drink. This diet that we call "dry fast" is the best for colloidal type's persons.

By drying up the humors, it allows the viscosities to pull out from the lymph and go through the blood circulation that will take them to the best elimination system.

The third way to fast, is to combine a dry fast plus a liquid diet, according to the patient's constitution, needs and possibilities.

Knowing that, whatever the kind of fast the person chooses, she must be guided by a trained professional.

How long can we keep fasting?

This will be decided with the professional coach according to the patient's constitution, and other criteria. The older, weak, and sick the person is, the shortest and more frequent should the fasts be.

One or two days per week, for example, or two or three days per months. Long fasts should be reserved for the strongest constitutions.

Do we have a functional constitution?

In such a case, we can easily with no harm, follow a liquid fast for several days, or even one, two or three weeks.

Knowing that even with the best constitution, the dry fast must not be longer than 3 days for a trained patient, but may last for five, six or even seven days for a strong and very experimented person.

Do we have a lesional constitution?

Then the best will be to make short and repeated fasts. A one to three days of liquid fast for example, could be repeated during the detoxification process, and repeated each week, each two weeks, or each month, depending on the patient's vitality and possibilities.

For longer periods, it is highly recommended to have a professional coach, same for the dry fast and mixed ones. The best criterion to know if we can continue to fast, is that we should not feel tired. On the contrary, we should feel more energized.

Let us conclude by saying that fasting is a perfect answer for the functional constitutions' crises. It may be less interesting for the lesional constitutions and has to be monitored by a specialist for the degenerative constitutions.

Those degenerative constitutions could actually feel a lack of energy, and not be able to eliminate the toxins that

open up during the fasting period; risking to provoke a dire self-poisoning.

It also means that even if fasting is a necessary technique for a healthy life, having a beneficial effect on the physical, psychological, mental and spiritual level, it also requires, and especially at the beginning, to be guided by a skilled professional.

We all know that a good morale helps the healing process, whereas fear often leads the patient to his ruin. Not only the patients' morale but also his relatives'.

"Fasting is like surgery without a scalpel", Dr Yves Vivini used to say.

Student of Dr Bertholet, a Swiss physician who left us a wonderful book about fasting that he always proposed to his patients, Dr Vivini created during the 1960's a fasting clinic, firstly in Longwy, and then in the Pyrenees mountains, and then in the Balearic islands.

Despite the amazing healings that he obtained, he had the worst difficulties with the French government, who would have the best interest to support him though. Tired of fighting, he died rather young, leaving a precious book which name was firstly "*Guérir par le jeûne*" (ndt: Healing with fasting) and after being rewritten.

It became "La bouffe ou la vie" (ndt: "*Grub or life*")!

Fasting and resting were always the major animals' techniques and ancient doctors, who did not know as much science as today, but were good observers.

We also need to mention that there are rules to be followed before, during and after a fast.

Whether it is liquid, dry of mixed, it must be prepared several days in advance. Two to three days before the fast, one has to take an evening purgation. It will show its effect the following morning and has to be completed with an enema after going to have a bowel movement. During two to three days, we will prepare and eat a "cellulosic mush" (boil some watery vegetables: salads, leeks, carrots, turnips, celery, **without any potatoes or fat, nor salt**). Throw away the water three times until only the fibers remain, to which you can add some herbs, according to your taste.

It will do like a grater to peel off the crust and varnish still attached to your bowels. The mush is perfect for constipated persons to whom and according to their need, one can add a laxative, a purge, or another enema.

Any fast correctly done, must end by a very progressive food intake, and even better, with lacto-fermented vegetable juice to regenerate the microbiota.

During the fast, if the person is strong and has no disease, she can continue to be physically active (gym, walk, jogging, slow sports, swimming etc.). But she should rest her brain.

And if she suffers and goes through an elimination crisis, she needs a total rest, so that, all her energy can be dedicated to the elimination and healing process.

As soon as there is the slightest smell of ether or acetone, or if the person is very nervous and makes nightmares, or if she feels extremely weak, it is wise to immediately stop the fast and slowly, very slowly… give her food, before she tries again.

Short and repeated fasts better clean the body and are better than long periods that only very strong constitution persons can successfully do.

In that case, persons with a degenerative constitution, should do only mono-diets, which will both, save their digestive function, and supply them with a specific nutritional intake.

A mono-diet means eating one single food per day. Like a fast, a mono-diet can be liquid, dry or mixed.

We call it liquid when it is made of vegetable fresh juice, whose minerals will be extremely precious for all the crystalloid types who are always demineralized. Or, made with sauerkraut juice or lacto-fermented vegetable juices, very well for persons with respiratory conditions or constipation. For whom prune juice is also very beneficial.

It can also be made with

- Dry and sweet fruits for those who love sugar and treats and for people with depressive tendencies
- Citrus fruits that they can mix
- Leeks or vegetable juices if they have blood circulation problems

The most famous mono-diet is the grape diet, particularly interesting for the thick blood persons.

Please note, that whatever mono-diet you choose, it will be good for you if you enjoy it.

Talking about a dry mono-diet, it is made with solid raw or cooked food that needs to be carefully moisturized with saliva to liquefy, and eaten in very small quantity, and only each time we really feel hungry or thirsty.

The most famous dry mono-diet is the rice mono-diet, simply made with rice cooked in water and that we eat just a teaspoon at a time. As for me, I prefer a sprouts' mono-diet. Both are mostly interesting for people who tend to swell.

Fresh fruit juice is especially recommended for persons with psychological or sentimental problems.

Apple puree mono-diet is rather for persons who need to shrink

Green mush diet is a real sweeping of the bowels

Lacto-fermented vegetables diet is good for people with lazy intestines

Whatever your choice will be, remember to fully salivate at each solid bite or liquid mouthful if you want to really take advantage of this mono-diet that differently from a fast, you can do anytime you want.

Despite all the advantages of fasting or doing mono-diets, you will frequently hear that it is important to eat well when you are ill, to get energy. This ineptitude gets more vote than fasts, purges, and mono-diets.

The results as well.

I need to say that, if fasting is the most ancient technique in the animal and human kingdom, it is also, with food, the less respected. Even if Jesus himself told us that illness can only disappear with fast and prayer.

Let me tell you this experience I did one year after my husband died. At the same time, I also lost the presence of my children scattered all around France for their studies; and also, our property in *Bief*, a charming small village of France, and everything attached to it.

Christmas time arrived, and for my pleasure, we were all together. But the day after, when they told me that, like every year, they were going to ski between Christmas and New Year's Eve, I felt so lonely and despaired that I decided to go on a strike. Which means that I decided to go to bed and fast. I had done well, because, if the two first days were terribly difficult (I did not know purgation yet), the third day I could take a book and as if by chance, it was:

"MAN, THE UNKNOWN" ("L'homme cet inconnu" in French) by Alexis Carrel, that I finished on the fourth day. And what a surprise when I woke up on the fifth day, happy and singing, with an energy I had not felt since long.

No drug or technique could have done better and faster

What happened?

Had my husband come back from the after-life?

Had my children come back?

Had my Bief property been given back to me?

No, nothing like that had happened. I had just offered my cells a cleansing experience, which had allowed them to reach higher frequencies. Amazed by the power of fasting, this ancient technique, I realized the crucial role it played on our functioning.

And also, why the psychotherapy classes are always at the end of the naturopathic syllabus and not at the beginning. The essential for this discipline, not being to analyze or dissect the low, destructive, and painful ideas, apparently coming from an unhappy childhood, a betrayal, a theft, or a loss that we cannot deny.

But the essential is to understand that we can only create and attract all bad and destructive things happening in our lives if we are linked to low and reverse frequencies. And that the best solution to free ourselves is to do what is necessary to connect with the highest frequencies.

Purges

If you went to Sunday school when you were a child, as I did, you probably learnt that

Before leaving Hell to enter Paradise, we must go through Purgatory.

Another idea that troubled the little girl I was and made me laugh the day I understood the great value of these forgotten and criticized "purges". When all that is needed is to take the right purgation, at the right moment, then we understand the meaning of the word Purgatory.

Hell is not a country, like I believed as a little girl, but a suffering state, when our deficient and poisoned cells can only connect to their reachable frequencies. Which will be all the lower and more destructive, the more deficient and poisonous they are.

Paradise is a state of well-being, happiness, peace, creativity, to which our well-oxygenated cells, properly nourished, remaining in a clean, if not pure environment, allow us to have access. **This state in which we are not wreckers of ourselves nor others, but co-creator of the Universe.**

It changes all!

This explains the interest to cleanse our humors, in other words to cross the Purgatory by purging ourselves. The aim of a purge, is not only to drain our bowels, but also to drag out a maximum residues from the "humors"; that, because they lack of energy, our body wasn't able to eliminate by the natural pathways.

So, it stored them in our deep humors.

It means that a purge enables us to quickly connect with higher frequencies, and therefore heal quickly and easily.

All the populations who live close to Nature, naturally use purges, like Native American Indians do during religious ceremonies, with purgative plants. Their acute sense of observation taught them that the cleaning made with these plants, not only kept them in good health, but also helped them connect with the Great Spirit.

Animals too, naturally purge.

If you observe a dog, who usually lives locked up, the first thing it does outside is eat grass to purge.

And as Dr. Vivin used to say: ***"It is not enough to put new furniture in a dirty house to make it nice to live in, one must also clean it".***

And so, feeding our body correctly is not sufficient to recover a good health, we must also clean the inside.

It is useful and necessary to purge. Sorry to repeat, but purging does not only consist in emptying our intestine from the matters inside, but also in activating our elimination system. So, it can remove the reduced, lyophilized toxins, accumulated in every hidden corner of our organism, and eject them.

Purge enables a deep cleansing.

Even if, as I often hear, purge did not work. The most important thing is not to provoke an intestinal or urinary storm; but to evacuate a maximum of old residues, not especially big. Because the life intelligence reduced them to the smallest, in order to store them in the body.

Still, even if it is and interesting and useful technique, let us not forget that a purge is a sort of intrusion to force our body. So, let us use it but not abuse of it.

Considering our misunderstanding of the elimination process of residues, we may be afraid that purgation damages our intestines. As soap or detergent can sometimes damage dirty fabric, a purge can possibly somehow deteriorate our bowel's secretions.

But is it a good enough reason not to wash laundry when it is dirty or to refuse a purge when you need it?

The dirt, in which we would leave our humors, cells and laundry, would ruin them more certainly than the soap, detergent or purge that clean them.

Among two harms,

In the old time, people used to purge a lot. As I was friend with my village pharmacist, she lent me a "Dictionnaire Vidal™" (French dictionary of medicines) of the 1800s, in which I discovered no less than 174 kinds of purge.

I prefer smooth and repeated purges to drastic harsh and violent remedies. In any case, a purge must be adapted to the nature of the crisis and to the energetic resources of the patient, who should never feel tired that much. In this case, we will replace purgation by another technique that we will see later. Meanwhile, as we have two natural elimination pathways and two sorts of residues, there are also two kinds of purges. One is called saline's purge and based on magnesium salts, the other is oily.

The saline's purges are made to solve uric acid of the crystalloid types and the oily purge to eliminate mucus of the colloidal types.

Let me tell you that the most loaded the urines are, the more they eliminate uric acid. So, the more they are beneficial and healing.

Everyone who comes from the South of France, know how good it is to swallow a spoon of olive oil every morning, to help cleansing the liver and the gallbladder.

Note that olive oil has nothing to do with castor oil, made to drag out the old mucus which stick to and plugged everything they touch.

Kidneys, for example, who cannot separate and evacuate the uric acid from the venous blood. It is easy to understand that the uric acid that is not eliminated, will return into the arterial blood circulation. Thus acidified, it will maybe one day cause a hemorrhage, exactly like when you pour acid in a pipe.

Besides, like the river drops the sand in each meander where the course slows down, the acidified blood will drop some tiny crystals of acid in each part where it flows slower (joints, inter-vertebral spaces, endocrines', or gallbladder...).

And each time it tries to get rid of them, you will experiment pain.

The first purge I recommend is "*Chlorumagène™*", that you can find in a drugstore. It will support your immune system as well as trigger an intestinal draining.

The second one is called in France "*Magnésie San Pellegrino™*", which you will also find in a drugstore and can choose in a regular or effervescent formula. I like it better regular. The effervescent one can flow all over but in your glass...

How to take a purge?
Every purge is done on an empty stomach, in the morning or replacing the evening dinner.

For Chlorumagène™

For an adult, take 2 full soup spoons in a glass of water and then, drink in the following 2 to 3 hours, 34 to 50 us fl oz (1 to 1.5 liter) of herbal tea, or water or vegetable broth if it replaces the dinner.

DO NOT EAT anything until you have a bowel movement.

Then take a tiny well chewed quantity of sauerkraut, or a small glass of lacto-fermented vegetable juice if you are constipated or enjoy a piece of your favorite fruit.

For Magnésie San Pellegrino™

For an adult, put 2 full soup spoons in a glass of water and drink, in the following 2 to 3 hours, 34 to 50 us fl oz (1 to 1.5 liter) of herbal tea with hydrosol or vegetable broth.

DO NOT EAT anything until you have a bowel movement.

Then, take a tiny well chewed quantity of sauerkraut, or a small glass of lacto-fermented vegetable juice if you are constipated, or a glass of fresh fruit juice.

Note that, if your urines are pale as water, it means that your kidneys are full of viscosities and cannot eliminate the uric acid, which will go back into the arterial circulation, leaving some residues in the slow parts along its way. Expect to suffer from all possible pains.

For castor oil

In case you suffer a lot, I recommend to take some **castor oil[1] prior to the treatment,** because it cleanses your kidneys enough to have colored urines, meaning that they eliminate the melting acids that cause you pain.

Castor oil has been used for ages to loosen and expectorate mucus and phlegm which are at the origin of all colds, sinusitis, bronchitis, asthma, anxiety, dark thoughts, and diseases as well and annoying troubles, sometimes painless... Without forgetting tumors...

For an adult, put 3 to 5 full soup spoons of castor oil (start with 3 and take more if it is not sufficient) in a half glass of grapefruit or pineapple juice, even bottled juice; and if you have a juice extractor, in fresh apple juice with ginger.

Then take 2 drops of peppermint essential oil, or another one if you prefer.

DO NOT EAT OR DRINK until you have a bowel movement.

Because mucus is not soluble in water, so to drain them from the lymph into the blood circulation, it is important to dry up the liquids in which they are stored.

1. Castor oil is a powerful laxative, follow the advice of a health practitioner before any internal use, especially for pregnant women.

So, drink very little that day and only take small quantities of your favorite fruit or some lacto-fermented vegetable properly chewed with saliva.

For sick children, suffering from bronchitis asthma, rather than drink the castor oil; I recommend wrapping them every evening with a castor oil poultice that they will keep all night long, until they get better. And even a few days more if necessary.

Put on the little belly a thick layer of castor oil largely spread, and quickly cover it with a wool linen or some cotton wool. Then fix it with a Velcro band and make sure that he can move without removing the whole thing. Until he gets better, leave him on a diet or mono-diet of soaked prunes, orange juice, or vegetable or fruit juice that he likes.

The following day give him a shower and rub his chest with a few drops of eucalyptus essential oil and every evening do the wrapping again as long as your child is sick.

Remember that when we are sick, it means that our body asks for help to liberate from the toxins we have introduced by eating improper food, not the one that nature has planned for us.

This wrap can also be made during 2 or 3 months for adults suffering from chronic diseases. (ndt: please read "*Edgar Cayce's Quick & Easy Remedies*").

The best interest of these treatments is to find and eliminate all the residues stored and hidden each time we were sick. Hoping to be healed, we took drugs and prevented our body from eliminating.

This is how castor oil does wonders, for all the kidneys loaded with mucus and also for the persons with a respiratory condition. It is the same for anxious, shy, obsessed or even suicidal persons, because their psychological and mental illnesses are, before all, due to this colloidal overload which froze or slowed the nervous connections.

A real healing can only be done this way.

How can I resist to the testimonial I received this morning?

"I am staggered... For the last two days, I have been incredibly anxious. I took 3 spoons of castor oil and after a few minutes, I saw my enthusiasm come back!

Why?

How?

It doesn't matter, I recovered my energy!

What an electroshock, that moment of disgust!

But what an immediate well-being!

Thank you, Irene, who knows where my anxiety could have led me.

I have hundreds of similar testimonies.

If you feel down, simply do the same as this man and you will be convinced.

More generally, we can say that castor oil is the remedy for colloidal types and saline's purges are the one for crystalloid types.

But do not forget, if kidneys are blocked with mucus, even for the crystalloid types, they can take all the purge they want, it will do nothing. Nothing until they have started with the castor oil protocol that will liberate them from the mucus which blocks the kidneys' functions.

Just like it happened to this young man, asthmatic since his childhood, who had a severe accident when he was 14, with two skull fractures, another one of the clavicle, a broken right femur and left femoral neck.

Of course, he had surgery. His left femoral neck got a pin, the femur of the other leg a bone screw which hurt him so bad that he had to remove it quickly. The skull fractures and the clavicle healed by themselves. Knowing my methods, he used to take a purge every time he suffered and got better after.

One year, even with the purge and fast that always helped him, his pain did not stop. Not understanding what was happening I used radiesthesia and sent him to an osteopath who liberated a nerve and the pain stopped.

Happy with this method, that he found easier than purge, the following years he continued to use osteopathy.

One day though, and this is where I wanted to take you, even with the manipulations and drugs that he had started to take, the pain was so intense that he could not sleep. Going back to the old traditional methods he took some purge with magnesia, but it did not work, so he came back to me.

Four days with castor oil, a dry fast, some rest and he could sleep again without pain.

His pale urines had told me that his kidneys were overloaded with mucus, created by the asthma from his childhood. They could not get rid of the uric acid.

In general, saline's purges dissolve and evacuate excess of acidity, and should be used every time we have fever, otitis, tonsillitis, or any other physical or psychological painful manifestation.

Same for the women with painful periods. They should take a purge two or three days before the date. Especially if they choose to replace meat and dairy products with fruits, salads, and vegetable juices.

I recently discovered

"*The amazing liver and gallbladder flush*" written by Andreas Moritz, and I am going to try it, because it seems to be a perfect additional technique to castor oil.

As a conclusion, we will remember that saline purges with magnesia salt, are amazingly beneficial to all physical, psychological, and mental pains. Oil purges are rather for people with cold, bronchitis, asthma who are shy, anxious, and slow colloidal types.

When and how should we take a purge?

Knowing that a purge requires a lot of energy, we will avoid mealtime but rather take it in the morning on an empty stomach or even better, instead of the evening dinner.

Which frequency?

Every time we feel bad, and also in spring or autumn, like they did in the ancient times.

Or each week, each two weeks, to recover from a chronic condition. In this case and according to your therapist, it will be preceded or followed by a short fast or a mono-diet of your choice.

Also remember to drink as little as possible with castor oil, since the mucus are not soluble in water.

The best to do, is go to bed with a hot water bottle placed on the liver and the feet, especially if your feet are cold.

I personally rarely purge children or seniors, to whom I rather counsel castor oil wrapping. For the simple reason that purge requires more energy and if we use it for a weak person, it could have dangerous consequences.

The main interest remains to help our body get rid of its residues, rather than stop the process, each time we feel bad.

Because when they are locked down deeper inside our body, our poisoned cells will continue to ask for the "poisons" which created the residues in which they live.

And this will poison us ever more, preparing our body to suffer from not only functional but rather lesional or degenerative illnesses.

Because the liquids in which our cells are immersed are saturated with residues which penetrate the cells and:

- Either they **deprogram their brain** and create a cancer
- Either they will **sclerose** it and we will have a multiple sclerosis or diabetes
- Either they will **paralyze** it, which will give Parkinson disease or any another paralysis
- Or they will **disconnect** it and we will be suicidal or murderous.

So, we should consider and treat our body like this fantastic laboratory aimed at Loving, Thinking and Acting that it is, and simply live according to Nature, who offered us to make our own life

A HAPPY AND SUCCESSFUL LIFE!

For which nature gave us all.

Water and its use

According to what we now know, it is impossible to live without breathing or drinking.

As we all know, the best beverage for all the living creatures on earth is water.

Not a pure water made in a laboratory, out of oxygen and hydrogen molecules, but true, vital, natural water that Nature offers us.

French engineer Marcel Violet showed us that frogs bred in chemically pure lab water had no chance to survive. Whereas the tadpoles kept in a sealed container previously passed through an oxygenated current and exposed to the sun rays, lived normally.

It means that the bacteria-free water given by the chemist is improper for life. Especially when it contains alkaline substances (like bleach) meant to kill the living germs and microbes. The chemically purified water from our tap has nothing to do with the water that living beings need. The living water contain germs useful to our intestinal functioning.

According to Pierre-Valentin Marchesseau, the chemical treatment of water is an anti-biotic process, in the proper sense of the word meaning "opposite to life".

Whatever the chemists say, water from the tap containing bleach to destroy the streptococcus, enterococcus, vibrio's and other fecal bacteriophages and salmonellas, is no proper drinking water. So, in order to neutralize this aberration, they recommend using a device that mechanically filters and eliminates foreign substances, dead bacteria, or excessive chlorine.

Device that make a purer water used for drinking, herbal teas, soup, ice cubes or skin care... even for babies.

But even though it has been filtered, this water will never equal the natural water which received the sun ray's energy and went through clay and rock layers in the soil.

To fairly understand the importance of water in our body, note that it is made for one third of cells, and for the other two thirds of liquids. These constantly need to be renewed with the only liquid able to take on this function:

WATER, the only true beverage for human beings, animals, and plants.

Water, that not only fulfills our daily needs, but also cleans our body fluids though processes that have been implemented for thousands of persons with a constant efficiency.

Processes that in themselves, could need an entire book but among which we will only reveal the most interesting ones we know.

Again, according to Pierre-Valentin Marchesseau, the least known but most efficient treatment is the thorough internal body cleansing, which conjugates both distilled water intake of Dr Hanish, intestine shower of Dr Pfleiderer and fasting therapy of Dr Bertholet. The addition of these three techniques is beneficial for 60% of us, and provides the cleanliness that heals, said Louis Khune.

Other multiple water techniques can be used for maintenance, improvement, or recovery of a healthy condition. Among others, we can mention the Indian technique "*shanka prakshalana*" called in French "*circuit inversé*", in case of intestinal bowel obstruction, without requiring surgery, a great yogi cleansing.

According to Dr Bertholet, deep enterocolitis could improve as well as stubborn constipation, with only one single bowel cleansing. The main rule is to use cold water and enough pressure for constipated persons and warm water with less pressure for the diarrheic.

We will also mention colonic irrigations and enema which have no counter indication, except hemorrhoids crisis, which require to thoroughly oil the cannula and insert it gently into the rectum. It will not be done though for persons with colon cancer.

Colon and rectal cancer being among the most common, it is easy to understand the interest of these two techniques to prevent them. It seems that they could, alone, reduce the cases by half.

Colonics and enemas leave an incredible sensation of well-being. It should be counselled to insomniacs because it improves the sleep, or for women conditions, combined with a vaginal shower.

The addition of these two techniques considerably extends youth and beauty.

Let us also take a glance at all the little techniques that may help us, like nose, throat or eyes cleansing. We will only clean ears in case of severe pain, and stomach in case of food or drugs intoxication.

So many ways that all civilizations in the world used them, since the dawn of times, to clean their body or parts of it. So did the Moor, the Turkish or the Romans, among the most popular.

They all used bath to wash and also to isolate from the disturbing vibrations, going back to the fetal-like environment. It could explain the enthusiasm that people always showed for baths.

In the beginning of the 20th century there were two major tendencies:

The first one teaching,
Hot and very hot baths, with Dr A. Salmanoff, that pleased the nervous types to which he belonged.

The second one,
Local and cold baths of priest Sebastien Kneipp, perfectly suited hot sanguine temperaments like he was.

This explains the equal success of those two technics apparently opposed.

Like most therapists do, each of them proposed the type of bath that best suited him.

Hot bath to warm up the retracted, cold sensitive temperament like this tall and slender Dr Alexander Salmanoff. And cold bath to cool down the inner fire caused by the acid meats and delis or alcohols that the fat, swollen and sanguine temperament like Sebastien Kneipp preferred.

The modern pediatrics recommends a bath, two to three degrees below the body temperature for a child with fever. This prevents the temperature from raising too high and cause damage, while the child can still evacuate his poisoned heritage. This method is certainly better than the one consisting in hiding and drowning the causes of the illness with medicines.

I personally use the "derivative bath" of Dr Louis Khune.

This great 19th century's naturopathic doctor who, besides the diet change that he taught to all his patients, recommended some baths techniques, among which the famous derivative bath or hip bath with friction. This technique provides an immediate cooling inside the body heated by fever, while it also activates the intestinal and renal functions. During the winter it has to be done in a room where the temperature is pleasant, and only on a small part of the body. The patient should feel a nice sensation of warmth.

How to do a derivative bath with frictions?

Fill up a basin with smooth edges, with water as cold as possible, and place it over the toilet bowl. You may add ice cubes to the water if it is not cold enough, knowing that the coldest the water is, the most efficient the bath will be. Except when women having periods, they, or the little girls, will sit on the basin and gently and continuously scrub their genitals with a washcloth soaked with the coldest possible water.

Men and boys will hold the penis in the water with one hand, while lifting the skin covering the foreskin and rubbing it with a washcloth soaked in the coldest possible water, with the other hand.

Each time this bath is given at the beginning of the crisis, it reduces the temperature by two or three degrees within ten minutes. In case the crisis is already advanced, it will not reduce it but increase the temperature. It does not mean that the bath should be stopped. On the contrary, it must be continued for one or two days to restart the elimination process with which the fever will end.

The derivative bath with friction will be made during ten to twenty minutes and started again each time the fever raises.

As this technique helps the person to fall asleep, he will use all his energy to eliminate. **Of course, if the patient falls asleep, which help him to increase his energy level, we must wait until he wakes up for the next bath**. He will probably want another one, after having heavily sweated or feel an urgent need to pee or move his bowels. He could be very thirsty and will drink only water or herbal tea. The person will, of course, remain on a diet and purge if necessary. The derivative bath will always speed up the recovery.

Why do we use this part of the body?

Because it is one of the most accessible parts, that contains many nervous ramifications and can be invigorated and revitalized with cold water by a reflex with the parasympathetic nervous system.

This kind of parasympathetic therapy, which soothes the glandular and nervous system, is particularly efficient for persons with fatigue and stress. Especially when it comes with a series of hyper hot baths, steam or sweating techniques which enhance the elimination of the uric acid through perspiration, said Dr Louis Khune.

Let us also mention that hot bath followed by cold ablutions, massages, and exercises, always improve the varicose veins. Even better if the patient is on a specific diet.

This "W S M" method: Walk, Sweat, Massage, always brings out excellent results.

So many misconceptions haunt our minds while nature fulfills all our needs with its treasures, helping us repair our mistakes and have a better life. There are a number of hot springs offered by nature that have interesting properties.

Like, in France,

Chaudes-Aigues in the French area "Cantal": Chaudes-Aigues means "hot water" in old local dialect, with a 180°F (82°C) water, known to cure rheumatism, sciatica and other ankyloses.

Plombieres, in the Vosges Mountains, reserves its nurturing 158°F (70°C) hot water to persons suffering from neuralgia and colitis.

Battaglia in Italy, with a 156°F (69°C) spring water, is also the right place for these affections.

Baden-baden, in Germany, is especially recommended for skin and female genital diseases, with its 154 °F (68°C) water.

For dermatosis and rheumatism pains, we have **Evaux, in the Creuse region**, with its 134°F (57°C) spring.

And for the same symptoms, you could go to **Néris, in the Allier** which has water reaching 125°F (52°C).

Many others, like **Sylvanos, in the Aveyron** and **Bains-les-Bains in the Vosges,** once more recommended for dermatosis, pains and genital diseases.

If the scientific approach pretends that these waters have a therapeutic effect because of the natural radioactivity and the elements they contain, let us consider thermal waters are perhaps also effective thanks to the heat rather than for their components.

Actually, we could do "home balneology" by simply adding these components to the water into our bathtub. The water would have to be hot, even very hot, like in a "hyper thermal" bath that only the persons able to sweat can tolerate. Those who do not sweat are more likely to faint.

How to take a hyper thermal bath?

Fill up half of the bathtub with water at the temperature that you like. Then immerse yourself into the bath, letting hot water pour, as hot as you can tolerate it. You can sometime pause and turn off the tap before you let the water run again until perspiration drops on your forehead.

If you feel any discomfort, be ready to get off the bath-tub and lie on a thick towel that you previously laid next to you.

Fainting can only arise when we lack energy for the elimination process. Our organism then, has to use all its resources to sweat.

We generally only need two or three minutes to feel better. The danger being to fall and hurt oneself if we feel weak.

This is why people who cannot sweat will not chose hyper thermal bath or sauna, but rather go to the steam bath. This steam bath opens the skin's pores, which allows the sweating process. In any case, this technique must be done very carefully **and under surveillance if you are a beginner.**

Hyper thermal bath is a blessing for the retracted, nervous, and painful persons, who can enjoy them largely, as long as they sweat.

On the counterpart, cold ablutions of the great practitioner, Sebastien Kneipp, a Bavarian healer, also known as the private butler of the Pope and Commander of the Holy Sepulcher, are beneficial to the hot sanguine persons, as he was. He demonstrated the interest of cold-water applications on hot bodies.

Mr. Kneipp quickly understood that, by walking or taking hot steam baths, his patients interestingly felt hot. Then he rubbed them, in order to bring the heat to the skin, then finally soak them with cold water that he poured with a watering can, swinging like a pendulum over the hot body. It could be any part: knees, arms, thighs, chest or back. This **"hot to cold"** technique is a sort of blood circulation gymnastics' that every good practitioner should know.

As a conclusion, I will say that bath always help the recovering from any illness and keep us healthy, if used properly. So, we should not neglect them.

To be practical, starting the day with a Scottish shower will wake us up and will be much more efficient and less dangerous than coffee. Still, in the beginning, you could have both.

How to take a Scottish shower?

We will start by keeping our feet in hot water, take a long warm shower and then finish with cold water quickly running over the whole body. We can do this as often as we like. People from Northern Europe use to roll into the snow after a sauna because a hot body cannot feel the cold. Whenever it is possible, I recommend taking a weekly steam bath, it can be sauna or Hamman, because when opening and cleaning our pores, we strengthen our skin and allow it to sweat.

Let us not forget that **these techniques are only interesting for people who can perspire.**

If not, theses bath could be dangerous and should be replaced by hot tubs, Californian baths, or Jacuzzi, usually not more than 97°F (36°C).

Animals naturally take mud bath when they like or whenever they are wounded. Whereas we can do a clay body wrap or an herbal bath in a spa.

In related techniques, we have cold hand or forearm baths which are strong derivatives, as Mr. Kneipp cold ablutions. German hot and dilated temperaments use them a lot.

For retracted nervous temperaments, we will prefer hot footbath, sometimes adding mustard flour. **Hot footbath is extremely useful and should be practiced by any person with cold feet.** We do them, starting with warm water at 100°F (38°C) that we slowly raise to 108°F (42°C). Feet should turn red at the end of the bath.

There is no better method to divert the blood in case of head congestion.

These types of hot footbaths are specifically beneficial for people with migraines, insomnias, or others with psychological and mental issues. We will find great benefits to combine them with enemas and fasting.

To make a mustard's flour footbath, which creates a hot effect using warm water, you will dilute mustard flour in a 98°F (37°C) water.

The beneficial use of poultices and warm compresses has unfortunately been replaced by antibiotics and other medical drugs. So, was it for the wrappings and clothes intended to take off congestion from certain parts of the body? Rika Zaraï, a famous French singer, used to promote the hip baths, saying that they were extremely good for people who, like her, prefer cold to heat.

To take a hip bath, also known as "perineum bath", use either a basin or a bathtub filled with water up to the belly button. It is similar to the Louis Khune derivative bath, which is harder to bear for fragile persons, but easier to use. It should be done progressively from 1 to 10 minutes, its main interest being the "negativation". The hip bath can be easily integrated in our daily routine.

Which is not always possible with the Lukewarm and continuous bath recommended by Baruch, that we would like to use in a spa, but is only proposed at the hospital. Baruch warm bath suited both severe burnt, agitated, or nervous persons of all kinds. And people suffering from long lasting and large skin affections (eczema, psoriasis, acne) or chronic insomnias. It also suited tobacco, alcohol, or drug addicts as well as patients refusing any kind of food (mental anorexia).

The long-lasting lukewarm bath seems to provide the best conditions of rest and rebalance for the neuro-vegetative system, resembling those of the baby in his mother's womb.

We will learn more during the professional classes that we are now offering for therapists.

But, remember that according to the laws of hydrotherapy, hot baths are recommended for neuro-arthritic types and cold baths for hot sanguine types.

~ ***And it is a matter of logic, so simple!*** ~

Let us notice that warm baths clean and cold baths revitalize.

Love, this essential guide to natural behaviors, will tell us which the right choice is for us, if we just do the type of baths we LOVE.

So, forcing someone who does not like it to take a bath, according to your own inclination, could be dangerous.

Physical exercises

There are two sorts of creatures living on earth: immobile or vegetal and animated or animal.

Like all other animated creatures, man has to move to find his food, whereas plants receive their own from the air and the soil and do not need to move in order to feed.

So, man is an animated live creature.

Movement is necessary for animated creatures; this is why they are called "*anim-als*". It facilitates their fundamental functions of breathing, nutrition, and elimination. Even the strongest people cannot resist the locking up of a sedentary lifestyle and get sick like wild animals who perish in their cage. In our over industrialized, mechanized, and robotized civilization, we are more and more deprived of our necessary movement. We then need to practice sports and gym, like human beings always did.

In the ancient Egypt, 5000 years ago, Herodotus thought that food and exercise were the two golden keys for health.

In China, gymnastics seem to be part of their origins. 3000 years BC the Tsao Tse monks codified the Kung Fu practice. Father Amiot brought it to the Occident in the 18th century. During the great and wise Greek period, the Academy of Pythagoras taught the disciplines of arts, exercises, and metaphysics. Greek gymnasiums were places to practice and teach. Antique Greek civilization is still our “top” in the idea of perfection. The Olympic Games were created in the Antique Greece where all sports were represented. Athletes were forced to play naked. An accomplished athlete had to follow a diet taught by Iccus, and Plato, Socrates and Plutarch considered Herodotus as the athletes’ doctor, with his medical gymnastics from which Hippocrates was inspired. In Rome, where obesity was considered an imperfection, the Romans combined practicing baths and sweating with their exercises.

But with a meat-based diet they started to eat, Roman’s Games soon became armed combats and cruel circus games; succeeded the pure and athletic traditions inherited from the Greek.

During the middle ages, the Church replaced sports with equestrian jousts, ball games and a precursor of rugby, played by the nobles. At the Renaissance, exercise came back with Symphorien Champier, Charles VIII’s doctor. Luther and

Rabelais sang its praises. Then later, Ambroise Paré and Montaigne continued to praise and to practice it.

Closer to us, Hippolyte Triat promoted physical exercise with dumbbells and was the pioneer of our contemporary bodybuilders.

Then Dr Edmond Desbonnet, gave gymnastics its credentials.

Not only because of its hygienic and medical impact, but also for its esthetic and athletic aspect. People like Mc Fadden in the USA, Eugen Sandow in England, Dr Von Krajewski in Russia; as well as Marcel Rouet or Jean-Edouard Ruffier in France, followed the same ideas.

Between the two World Wars, Marcel Rouet practiced bodybuilding while Pierre-Valentin Marchesseau preferred and developed organs' gymnastics, following Desbonnet's idea who said that ***"Physical training and sports were not made to develop our strength and compete but rather to develop and improve our weaknesses for a better life".***

He demonstrated that spinal gymnastics' use was not meant to fight against the stiffness of age but to correct the children's back deflections (bent back or scoliosis), to regenerate the intervertebral disks in case of rheumatic, cervical, dorsal, or lumbar pains and to facilitate their growth with stretching and growing-focused exercises.

Spine gym must be practiced either on a mat, on a table or suspended, straight or head down. He also promoted

Dr Louis Hasson's respiratory gymnastics, which he recommended to bronchitis, asthma, emphysema affected persons and to everyone fragilized with a respiratory condition. Respiratory gymnastics is meant to empty the capillaries and help the blood circulation returning to the heart.

He especially did abdominal exercises with persons having liver, stomach, and intestine conditions. This practice is done on a mat. It massages liver, gallbladder, stomach, intestine and colon by soliciting the abdominal and diaphragmatic muscles.

It tends to develop men's strength and power and women's grace and flexibility.

a) Strength comes with weightlifting and becomes power when combined with speed. Women do not need dumbbells, which do not correspond to their physiology but masculinize them. They need stretching exercises. They should also work on their vertebral joints, scapular and pelvis widenings, which will sculpt and shape them better than dumbbells.

b) Speed and relaxation come with fast running. **These qualities are rather meant for men than women.** Nevertheless, men over their 40s should be careful with speed and jumping exercises that can cause muscular tears on acidified persons.

c) Dexterity is a quality for both, and can be developed with a large range of exercises, like juggling, walking on a thread or a beam or target practices (archery...)

d) Resistance is essentially masculine and improves with long distance running, long bicycle ride or dumbbells practicing.

e) Flexibility is a quality for both sexes, mostly feminine. With stretching and uneven bars exercises, our modern gymnastics seem to be the best sport activity for women's needs, and when flexibility is enhanced by choreographies with rhythm and music; like in acrobatic dance and figure skating, we totally reach our goal.

Considering that building a healthy and beautiful athlete who developed features like strength, power, speed, dexterity, resistance, and flexibility, requires a lot of time; we shall remember that practicing exercise regularly and moderately always improves life's quality.

Nowadays our blind materialism's attitude does not help us chose that sort of thorough athletic culture but rather pushes us to choose sports which are often against our physiology and jeopardize our health, by only aiming to raise the human's machine efficiency.

It also builds wealthy champions who have their time of glory, until one day, when competition ends, they become sick.

This is a proof that developing one single aspect of the being, like in show sports and competition which are only motivated by money, is an error, and could be compared to the Games in the Decadent Rome.

"Panem et circenses" (Bread and games) was the motto of the Romans, spoilt by lust and money.

Let's hope that governors and governed ones will one day erase these nasty illusions: a cyclist who needs doping substances to pedal; a boxer who agrees to lose sight or turn mad under the blows, just for money; a rugby player putting his life at risk every Sunday; or a long distance runner who accepts to be scrawny to the bones to see his name on top of the list.

On the other side, the rational practice of sports like walking, running, cycling, playing tennis, skiing, swimming, playing soccer or weightlifting with friends etc. are very good habits to maintain our physical condition, our cardio-resistance and life extension.

And for those who want to do more and better, they should know that Desbonnet's moderate and progressive gymnastics, adjustable in intensity will always help their health, beauty, and strength.

The rules of this, are to lift light and medium weight dumbbells, breathe according to a precise protocol with an open glottis, and the attention paid to muscles, structure, and posture.

This is the original technique that all his followers used.

An exception is the American neo-bodybuilding school, whose teaching was based on heavy weights, resulting in hideous hypertrophies of the exhibition muscles, to the detriment of healthy muscles such as the paravertebral and abdominal muscles.

Competition is totally anti physiological and does not produce healthy, strong, beautiful, and happy people as they should be. But stressed, exhausted and deceit athletes who need to take doping substances to reach their goal.

A well-managed physical training should produce a gain of vitality, which shows with the resistance to illnesses. It makes men and women look more beautiful and also develops a number of significant aptitudes in gestures and bearing.

A correct practice of physical training also eliminates awkwardness and brings an acute awareness of the body, which has an influence on shy and emotional persons. Exercise will also improve self-confidence and a feeling of security that increase our social value on both human relationships and success.

The correct practice of exercise should masculinize men with muscles and feminize women by shaping them and making them more beautiful.

We could say that women's body, which shapes and unshapes faster than men's is made of clay, and men's body is made of iron.

Let's remember that the best gymnastics and sports are the ones for which we are the less talented, and the best way to consider athletics is an amateur and complete practice where the person will probably never be a champion, but will accomplish his life helping others.

So was the Greek ideal in their best time.

Sleep and relaxation

After effort comes comfort, or more precisely resting

According to our forefathers, sleep would be more restorative in the first part of the night than during the second. Because, in the first part, we regenerate our potential; and in the second, we prepare for the awakening. Probably the reason why they said that *"sleep before midnight counts for double".*

This quality of sleep was partly lost with the discovery of electricity. Whatever beneficial it is, it made us lose our best sleeping hours. We started drinking coffee or tea every morning instead of soup that our grandparents had. We took more stimulants and consequently more tobacco and medicines to relieve us. This awful duet could only end by feeling stressed in the first place and then down.

And there came depression, which many great coffee-drinkers experience. How many hours of sleep do we need?

It depends on our constitution and on our endocrine's quality.

Are these very strong?

Then four or five hours of sleep will be enough to feel fit.

Are they weaker?

We may need seven, eight, nine hours or even more to feel fit, but still need some coffee, tea, or chocolate to start our day.

According to Pierre-Valentin Marchesseau, the best we sleep, the less dreams we remember. Except if they were nightmares and reveal a functional disorder, or in case of premonitory dreams, which is a totally different issue.

The best is to fall asleep as we go to bed. If it is not so, we could believe that it is due to disturbing ideas and worries. But, in reality, they can only disrupt our sleep if we are connected to low frequencies. That is to say, when we are deprived and intoxicated by a poor-quality food and a bad maintenance of our humors.

We always get back to it!

Let me tell you, when I happen to have some difficulties falling asleep, I know It is time for a purge and one or two days of fast or mono-diet. After this, as if by magic, I instantly fall asleep in minutes.

It means that, like for all our problems, sleeping troubles come from the quality of our constitution and functioning. There is much better to do than take sleeping pills which will not really solve our problem but certainly get us addicted, for the greatest satisfaction of drug companies.

If we do not purge, we could at least start by avoid coffee, alcohol, tea, soda, and beer… as well as all preparations made with refined sugar. An evening meal consisting in fruits will be quite beneficial. We could also associate this vegetables and fruits meal with an evening walk to oxygenate our nervous system. And why not a nice warm bath and a friction with lavender essential oil followed by a lime, marjoram, lemon balm, verbena, or orange blossom herbal tea before going to bed.

We will certainly sleep better!

If ever this is not enough, we can take some plant supplements like "Ervorola" from Superdiet company, "Bonne Nuit" (ndt: good night) from Salus company, or maybe two or three pills of Griffonia or Saint John's Wort. A few drops of marjoram, chamomile, sweet orange essential oils can also be interesting. Nelly Grosjean, my oldest daughter, sells compositions called "NERôm" and "HARôm" from Biossentiel company; that you can swallow with a hint of honey in warm water or directly put on your skin.

Since none of these products creates addiction, we will easily stop taking them when we sleep better. And if we take them continuously for a while, they will help regenerate our nervous system.

If this is still not enough, we can take a fifteen- or twenty-minutes hot foot bath that will help us feel relaxed, especially if we breathe enough and deeply during the foot bath. We can also have nice thoughts, letting the hot water pour so that the foot bath does not cool down and its temperature raises as much as we can bear.

Still not enough?

In this case, we probably need some relaxation sessions as well as serious reform of our diet and a good fitness program. With all this you will sleep like an angel, whatever your problems are, for which you will soon find an answer.

Air, food, water, sleep, and rest are crucial for a good life.

All the world's religions have called for one day of rest a week, besides fasting and praying.

The aim of this habit is to use all the energy that we spend in work, to connect to the frequencies of life and consequently reach a higher spiritual level.

Instead of that, we have made of this holy day a moment of entertainment that, in the best case, we devote to sports and relaxation, and also to drive our car, see our friends with whom we enjoy good meals with lots of wine, and then go to bed ever later. Of course, the following Monday we feel more tired than before our resting day. Like the French singer Pierre Perret sang:

"If we are tired, we eat,
If we eat, we drink,
When we drink, we smoke,
And when we smoke, we are sad..."

We become more sensitive to sad ideas and feelings, and slowly drift towards depression, failure, conflict, separation, accident, or serious illness.

Will we take a few days of rest, and do what should be to recover? Or do we bow down in front of this new hassle that just arrived, without changing anything in our awful habits?

Doctors in the past, used to recommend this old fashion, still totally topical rule, saying that "**fast and rest are the basics of recovery**". Which reminds me of the center I have been dreaming about for a long time.

A real practical health school!

A school where people will rest right at their arrival, until they really feel like doing something. A center where, like this mother of six, everyone can rebuild their health at their own pace. This mother who, besides her six children and her business, had a very active participation in the church's community. Too much, way too much, so that we do not end up collapsing one day.

For what reason did she think of coming to Bief?

I do not remember, but in those days, when things went wrong, people used to knock at our door. This old mill's that we had transformed in 1967, to spread the two wonders that are life and happiness which necessarily comes with it.

These two wonders that we thought we had found and wanted to share with the greatest number.

When this lady arrived, we started by listening to her, then drew her a bath, massaged her with lavender essential oil and took her to bed with a nice soothing herbal tea. We continued to bring her a bottle of water and herbal teas until she really felt like getting up. Four days of diet and total rest. Four days to let go and two weeks to learn how to breathe, eat, eliminate, and think positive. So, when she left, she was splendid and radiant. Besides the nine or eleven pounds that she was happy to have lost; she had solved almost all her problems and understood that **willing to earn more, she risked losing all**.

This experience guided us to imagine a place where exhausted people could come and learn how to find their inner-self and live according to their constitution and the laws of life.

A sort of health practice school, until we would one day open a healthy holidays club...

This idea is now growing in Morocco, thanks to a Swiss doctor whom I met some twenty years ago; and who, after two months practicing my methods, decided to work with me. The idea was sowed and almost took shape in the Philippines, where he used to go as a student, to meet the Philippine healers. He was charmed by the climate and beauty of the Panglao Island and bought some coconut trees planted land facing the ocean. He took me there several times to visit the San Benito Farm, his luxury health center nested in the tropical forest.

I was thrilled by idea of being involved in this paradisiac place, and we prepared the agreement. We had three months before we signed the agreement. During this time, I realized that my children would remain in France, the Philippines are far away, so I would rarely see them, certainly not enough. So, I did not sign the contract, to the great disappointment of Doctor Gacond.

Reacting like a colloidal type, he stuck to his idea and three years later, he called me, saying that he had just bought another land. This time only two hours plane from France, so I could not refuse.

"In Morocco?" Did I say
"Yes, how do you know? "
"Well, that's what came to my mind".

And for the last eight years he has been digging a well, equipping the site and planting 2000 fruit and olive trees, so that it looks like paradise. He also built houses to receive 40 persons from the beginning. Cyril finally built this wonderful center that we long dreamt of and should open as soon as it is ready.

It is called "The Dunes of Guemassa": The gardens of health.

This place is meant to be an oasis of health! Everyone in this paradisiac garden, will find and learn how to practically use the best natural techniques **to Live Really Alive!**

I hope I will soon welcome you there and waiting until you have enough time to rest, I will teach you how to relax. It means teach you to calm down your brain so that it stops using all the energy that your "organic brains" need to fulfill their goals. That sort of relaxation that people doing fishing, music, painting, DIYs, and gardening activities naturally practice for their own pleasure. This attitude stops the energy leaks opened by worries, sorrow, regrets, and obsessional ideas that besiege us when we are connected to low frequencies. One can do these relaxation sessions with a sophrologist or using CDs. These moments of relaxation allow us to re-connect to higher frequencies, where the solutions of our problems stay. I read somewhere that Sir Winston Churchill was an enthusiastic user of relaxation, that he practiced several times a day. I also know a Canadian entrepreneur who is in a perfect shape and walks two hours a day in the forest, where he says he finds the ideas to grow his business.

Because unlike what people think,
relaxation is not a waste of time,
but rather the best way to save it.

Complementary techniques

As you know it now, *if we are the sole architects of our sufferings and illnesses, we are also responsible for our health and happiness*!

Our health, this treasure that we care for once we are to lose it.

Health, which is to our life what foundations are to buildings. As we have seen all along this book, it is wise to follow the main basic techniques, which I remind you, are:

Breathing, eating, sleeping, and eliminating.

When required, we can add fast, purge, use of herbs, essential oils or balneotherapy. Without forgetting the secondary techniques, like the use of gas with the precious ozone and oxygen, against asthma and severe respiratory conditions.

Liver and gallbladder cleansing are among the most important and powerful approaches to enhance our health. You will find them in the book of Andreas Moritz. There is also a fluidic approach, with hands-on-healing techniques, that can be compared to a flat car's battery plugged to a full one, to make the car run. Which will not fill up the car of course, but at least help it re-start.

If hands-on-healing is precious in case of energy need, it cannot cleanse our humors. Like for our little boy whom we would probably have lost without the help of the healer. There are also all sorts of manipulation techniques like osteopathy, chiropractic, physiotherapy, massage... that are precious to drive out and disperse the residual blockages. Same with reflexology, acupuncture, or the highly interesting light therapy with actinology.

All these techniques being quite beneficial if we use them properly, like Mr. Jourdain who did prose without knowing, we can use colors with chromotherapy, music with musicotherapy, manual work and ergotherapy and many others. But we must keep in mind that, if secondary techniques can help us cross a difficult period, they can never replace the basic techniques, so neglected in our modern society.

This is why, with the New Medicine which has to come, we will not use these techniques alone, as people do; but in addition to the four basics and fundamental techniques: breathing, eating, sleeping, and eliminating.

Like a house built on weak foundations cannot last, we cannot expect strong and sustainable results with the sole use of secondary techniques. Recovering a good health with natural methods sometimes requires a lot of time, and if it does not go as fast as we hope, it is still better than loosing health.

It is so simple

You may tell me that I did not mention thoughts and feelings, although they are essential in our lives.

I know because I have fairly good reasons for that!

A long, long time ago, when I applied to the naturopathic class, like you today, I was surprised that the psychology and psychotherapy courses came at the end of the year, rather than at the beginning. As he probably perceived from my silent thoughts, the founder of the school smiled at me and said:

"Yes madam!
It is like that!"
What did he mean?

In those days, I did not dare ask him. But since then I have had plenty of time to understand that if love and thinking create our lives, they also depend on the quality and functioning of our little cells.

So, in a good naturopathy school, the founder had to start with the beginning.

Because, as it is true that love and thoughts create all the elements of our life, it also means that to love and think we need a body and the cells which compose it. Just as we need a phone to call, a radio to listen to the news, and a television to watch the programs. Like the quality of communication depends on the quality of the telephone or radio or television we use, the quality of our feelings and thoughts also depend on how our cells work to fulfill their wonderful functions.

It is so simple, so logical, and so natural that we hardly understand why we did not do it.

During the last century, the pharmacist Emile Coué having understood that thought is creative, and he developed a method called "Method Coué" from which come all the technics and methods of positive thinking, personal development, NLP etc. That now grows on the market to meet an increasing demand.

"Thoughts and imagination are the first skills of man", he said.

This takes us back again to life's starting point, which lies, as you cannot ignore it anymore, in the quality and the functioning of the cells and humors our body is made of.

Are these cells strongly built and in perfect working order?

If we can connect to the frequencies of life, they will lead us to a higher state of consciousness, to higher feelings, to clear and creative ideas with the energy to carry them out, all this in a harmonious and strong body.

Are they fragilized and in poor working order?

Cells will link us to low frequencies, as low and reverse as they are weak, deficient, and intoxicated. Knowing that these low and destructive elements can only be attracted in our lives if we connect to low and reverse frequencies. The best solution is not only to undergo a psychotherapy but do what is necessary to connect to higher frequencies.

The frequencies of life, which we can find only over the clouds, where it is always sunny and where the solution of all our problems lie.

Since images are clearer than words, let us imagine that we go to the airport and take a plane. The sky is so low and grey that it could fall on our head. But as soon as we fly higher, the dark clouds look cottony and as white as milk, when we fly over them. Like the dark sky that was over our head turns blue and gilded with the sun once we are over the clouds, we can transform our negative painful, destructive feelings and ideas by simply changing their frequencies and turn them into positive, happy and creative feelings and ideas.

Our worries, fears and revolts melt away like snow in the sun, under the light of faith and love, that we can only reach

and keep thanks to the right functioning of our cells and humors.

This means that when we psychologically or emotionally suffer, even if we think that knowing the cause is necessary, searching in a previous life, in our childhood, in our couple, or for any reason, it is much better and effective to start with a few days of detox.

It will help us change the frequencies we use to think or feel, which means change our point of view and consequently, have higher, happier, more positive, and constructive feelings and ideas.

So that, we can find the solution to any problem or torment. Because there is always a solution to any problem. The true reason of all our sufferings and physical pains, of our psychological and emotional disorders, lie in the quality of our "humors".

How many unsaid, anger, separations, conflicts, and wars did bad humors create?

How many wonderful and paradisiac moments did we miss? We can hardly imagine! When we know that happiness creates a paradisiac atmosphere everybody loves.

Most religions try to raise the spiritual level of their believers by praying and singing. This is already something, considering that besides, some teach to fast one day per week and forty days per year.

But we have replaced fasting with medicines, and prayer by mental techniques or psychotherapies. If they are sometimes quite interesting for emotional destress periods, they can never repair our cells behaviors or connect us to higher frequencies. This is why these techniques are more interesting when they come with a few days of fasting and purgation, or a mono-diet.

Religions recommended fasting prior to prayer.

Didn't they always say, "fasting and prayer" and not "prayer and fasting"?

Yesterday I received a woman who, a few years ago, weighed a 220 pounds. She lost them by replacing cheese and pasta, that were her preferred diet, with fruits and mostly raw vegetables.

This transformation not only gave her a dream shape and an optimal weight, but also a gain of energy that her organism quickly used to eliminate her stored residues stuck in her humors. These residues had damaged her endocrines, kidneys, gallbladder, and other organs, and also ruined her nervous system with coffee and wine that she enjoyed.

She was addicted to her preferred food and stimulants which were, as we know, the worse for her, and also to cigarette which contains opiates providing her – still now – a sort of artificial well-being; especially after the excitation provoked by drinking coffee. This sort of diet could only feed her with negativity and lack of self-confidence. The worse being that her week-end parties seemed to make her forget everything. Friends, coffee, and alcohol gave her a momentary illusion of happiness.

Even if after the pleasure, came dis-pleasure.

This is how, wasting her nervous energy reserves, day after day, she became less efficient and finally lost her job.

Once again, her body had to eliminate her annoying residues to face this shock. But one day, when she was a little girl, her mother had given her a purge with castor oil. It was gym day at school, and while climbing up a rope, her bowels discharged, to her greatest shame.

So, she promised herself that she would never ever purge again.

She refused the purge that I recommend to all the persons who change their diet. It more rapidly cleans their humors. Doing her way would take more time to get rid of her toxins and would leave her tired.

Moreover, changing from solid to liquid state for elimination, her acidic crystals while burning the minerals that are necessary for the nervous system, prevented her from sleeping and recharge.

Her emotional and psychological state got more and more negative and reverse.

The elimination process of all her viscosities slowed her intellectual and nervous functions, and she more and more frequently suffered from procrastination and obsessional ideas like consider her incompetence, which led her to despair. Being enslaved by low frequencies she started to sink into a merciless denial and started to refuse even the idea of going out.

What to do in such a case?

The best would be, of course, to have institutions with a perfectly healthy confident and operational staff, who would gently help the patients connect with higher frequencies, and then become more positive and creative.

But, since we do not have that kind of clinic, we must understand that worrying for her will not help. The best is to entrust her with as much love as possible, to life intelligence, which only wants her happiness! At the same time, maybe take her to a healer to transfer her more energy, or perhaps to a hypnotherapist who will help her think differently. In any case, surround her with love, entertain her, highlight her inner value while encouraging her to practice sports, gymnastics, walking, dancing, painting, singing or anything she likes.

Everything possible, so that her newly oxygenated and re-energized cells can again stay in a clean, if not pure, liquid; and connect to higher frequencies.

We know that everything is made of vibrations that we constantly send and receive. An hour ago, I just called a friends' son who has been in Japan for the last two years for is work. He told me that at the same moment he was writing an email to tell me that it was his fifth day of fasting and he had not felt so well for such a long time with ideas clearer than ever.

~ *Was it chance?* ~

Certainly not, because chance does not exist which is the title of a book by K.O. Schmitt, that I recommended him a decade ago, and that he was reading again, among others like:

"*The four agreements*" by Dom Miguel Ruiz and "*The cosmic ordering service*" by Barbel Mohr.

Reading the second book allowed him, two weeks after having read it, to go and work in Australia and then in Japan, as he wanted to, when all his previous attempts had failed. Maybe calling him while he was writing me was just a coincidence, it is possible. But for me, coincidences do not exist as such, but as a production of our mind.

About this subject, you could read **Deepak Chopra's book "*Synchro Destiny*"** or others on the same subject... If we are careful, we will soon realize that we can surprisingly communicate through incredible distances without any other device than ourselves.

Even if since we developed technologies rather than telepathy, we can instantly talk to the person we want, by simply typing on a telephone or computer keyboard, and see her with a camera.

~ *Is it not amazing?* ~

Happy or sad?

Does it mean that theses vibrations exist, and that these wonderful techniques which allow us to send and receive them with super performant devices, could perhaps be just a reflection of ourselves?

One day as I was listening to the radio, a journalist who was interviewing the French singer Charles Aznavour, asked him what he would do if he had no more luck in his life. Charles remained silent, so the journalist asked the question again? and the singer still did not answer. Surprised, the journalist wondered why and then Charles said:

> ***"You must understand Mr., that I never imagine what I do not want to happen to me"***

Could imagination and thoughts be comparable to the plan that an architect gives to a foreman in order to build an edifice. We could think so.

“*Be very careful with what you think, it is the most important*” were my husband’s last words.

“*I always thought that I could leave once the children are adults. This is the time…*” did he add the day before he passed, nodding, though no sign could let us expect it.

When he was seventeen, he was medically condemned, but since he thought he was too young to die, he made a vow to Notre Dame of Lourdes, telling that he wanted a home, a wife and children and that once they were grown up, he could go. It happened exactly so. Was he aware of it?

No, I don’t think so, and if, I hope that he would have asked to live longer, because the gifts of life are unlimited, and it’s only our fears and doubts that prevent us from believing and achieving.

Our life is full of identical stories if we look carefully…

When I lost my husband, I was so despaired that I did not care for anything. It was so quick, I lost everything in a blink of an eye. We sold the property for almost nothing and even the death insurance did not work…

And I had exactly what I had programmed, that is NOTHING!

When my genitor proposed to my mother and asked her father, he had a fatal accident, so I never knew him. Despaired and overwhelmed with sorrow, my mother tried to drown herself. By chance her brother arrived on time to stop her. But the thought was created, and two years later, I drowned and almost died of bronchopneumonia caused by the cold water. With the doctor's dark prognostic, my mother made a vow to Saint Bernadette Soubirous (people used to do that in those days) and promised her that she would name her next child Bernadette.

Bernadette came and she drowned at the age of twelve. Coincidence?

Patrick Drouot, a famous physicist, says that powerful thoughts can cross through generations in order to come true.

This is why it is extremely important to be careful with what we think, say, and imagine. These things constantly influence our consciousness and subconscious, to attract and create in our life everything that we send.

We must be very careful and always try not to succumb to fear, rebellion or negative ideas. As you understand it, they will take us to the realm of suffering and destruction. On the contrary, like lovely fairies, faith, love confidence and patience and things that make us happy, can help us clear out of dead-locks and difficulties.

Faith's best definition is the one I read in a tough moment of my life:

Deny the evidence and believe in what we want

At that time, I must admit that did not really believe in this. But after years of experience I can confirm. Even if we do not always want what is good for us.

Like in this naïve but so enlightening story:

"Once upon a time a lumberjack lived in a forest. A fairy came one day and proposed to carry out three wishes. As he was hungry and loved black pudding that he scarcely ate that was what he asked. So, he received as much black pudding as he wanted and even more. Everything that he touched turned into sausage, so he got one on his nose. He ate until disgust and thought that if he had gold, he could buy everything he wanted. So, he received as much gold as he wanted and even more. Everything that he touched turned into gold, water that he drank, bread that he ate and even the wood that he burnt. Despite all this gold he was hungry, thirsty, and cold. Feeling so bad, he asked if he could have his third wish. Of course, said the fairy, but be careful, this is your last one. Don't worry, said the lumberjack, I only want to be like I was before we met. So it was. He returned to what he had and enjoyed it as never before".

We could think that if he had been better connected, he would have asked for the real treasures of life, health, love, peace, and abundance. Since we are not better connected than him, we chose to complain on our fate, chewing over our resentment, curse and revenge that grow just thinking about them. Moreover, wasting our time and energy in negative thoughts, we do not have enough to program the positive events.

When something goes wrong, said God to Neale Donald Walsh in his book "*Conversations with God*", change the way you think. It isn't clear!

We consciously or unconsciously program the bad things that happen to us. We can deprogram them the same way that they were programmed, and the way we want.

When I realized how powerful thoughts can be, I pinned a card over my telephone, saying each time I looked at it:

"If you were grateful for everything that life gives you, you wouldn't have any more time to complain."

This card reminded me that "Gratitude" is the most beautiful word of our language. And if I were given to raise more children, it would be the first word I would teach them.

This simple word opens us to this special state that in Sunday school we called a state of grace.

Even when we are helpless let us be grateful for all that is left to us and that we would never give for anything, rather than complain about what we do not have. Don't you think?

So, for what would you give the ones you love?

For what would you give your eyes, your ears, your legs, your arms, your hands, with which you see, hear, walk, and

kiss. And your mouth with which you eat and can say so many nice things.

Thank you,
thank you again!

Worrying for ourselves or for someone else, even in hard time, would knock them down even deeper.

What is left to do then?

Do what should always be done. Breathe deeply until we are more confident and smile to life. Life who guides us and knows better than us, what we have to endure to better grow. Like on that evening, after my husband had passed. I was waiting for a train to Avignon, when in my desperate heart came this prayer:

I cannot stand it anymore when all is dark,

The night is dark,

The train is dark and so is my heart...

If at least I was sure that "You" exist.

What guided to me to this coach, where one traveler told me that he was unemployed, his sister was disabled, and he had to care for his old mother? I do not know, but he moved me enough to find the words that he hoped to hear. He stood up to thank me and I saw that he was a short person.

Thank you, God,
once again you gave
me the answer!

How could I complain comparing my own life to that of this person forever meant to see others from their bottom.

I really could not, because if I were not a beauty, at least I was looking like any other. So, I thanked life with all my heart for all I had received. And when I arrived at around 4 AM, I wrote this man a letter to tell him that if he really believed, he would find a better job soon.

I slipped the letter in Marcelle Auclair's wonderful book "Le livre du bonheur" (ndt: *"The book of happiness")* and sent both to him. A book that I always recommend for happiness seekers.

To my great surprise, he came over a few months later to thank me, saying that I had been his fairy.

A fairy! I would love that!

But what else did I do but reprogram the belief in his desires? Nothing. The one and only fairy or wizard was himself. He, who stopped complaining about his fate, worrying about the worst. He, who believed in finding a better job, and did it.

Everyone around him saw his transformation, even the priest who wanted to read the book. But he only gave him the title, being unable to draw away from it.

Once again, I thanked heaven for this fantastic lesson and immediately decided to cease thinking about what I had lost and focus on what I still had. Firstly, my children, whom I had not seen since their father's death, and who had lost a mother at the same time, and then all the persons in need who would come to me.

I realized that whatever sad we are, there is always someone sadder than us. This, of course, is not a reason to compete with all the desperate in the world.

Of course not! The best we can do is to be happy for ourselves. Because the happier we are, the best we can share with others.

Before you harvest, you must sow. And if you want to get carrots, do not plant cabbage. So, if we want health, love and money, or fame and happiness, we must imagine ourselves healthy, beautiful, strong, rich and happy and also send as much love, happiness and gratitude as possible, to everyone around and even to the whole world.

And like all good gardeners, peck, hoe and remove weeds as they grow, we must breathe to painful feelings and thoughts and replace them with pleasant feelings and ideas. It does not mean that we should ignore what goes wrong, but better understand that when the sun rises, darkness fades away.

You just have to do the right thing
and the wrong goes away!

In order to receive, we first must give. So, let us give and give, always giving the best of ourselves.

It is much more pleasant than whine and complain. Focusing of good things is already a happy thought, so why not try?

In those days, I also met artists who painted with their mouth or feet. These life-heroes painted amazing pictures, worth the most famous masters, because of their hard work, courage, perseverance, and pugnacity.

Do we need to lose our arms and legs to give our best and offer the world reasons to rejoice and marvel?

Like this industry owner who had just gone bankrupt. One thing after another, his wife also left, so, thinking that he had lost everything, he was dragging his life about and one Summer morning a cripple on a wheel board, joyfully shouted:

"Nice day lad, isn't it?"

Surprised and stunned, he wondered how a cripple could seem so happy. He thought and kept on thinking until he realized that he really had no reason to complain, and immediately decided to go back to life. He had understood that wasting his time and energy whining could only make him feel worse and stop him from doing what he wanted. This would be a double failure, so we must adapt and take advantage of the circumstances. Like this American who bought a huge piece of land by mail order, and when he went to see his farm, there was nothing but stones and snakes.

What do you think he did?

Did he sue the estate agency to be reimbursed? Not at all, he used his means and energy to create a snakeskin transformation factory and earned a lot of money with it.

When you cannot have what you like, love what you have

Since I read this story, every time I am in a tough situation, I ask myself what I would do if I were this man? And if I do not know, I ask my inner guide to help me, what he always does.

This is why I always walk through life calm and confident.

Not confident about anything or anybody but trusting in "what" guides us. It also does not mean to wait and see. It is a real challenge saying:

"If you help yourself, Heaven will help you"

Sometimes helping ourselves can be to just let go, so that our limited point of view gives more space to the Universal Intelligence, which very well knows what we need to co-create our wonderful world.

Do we have communication problems?

Let us say and visualize the word "together" until any animosity disappears from our heart. And then let us send as much love as we can, imagining that we are in good terms.

Is it a sentimental problem?

Rather than whine for ourselves and feel resentment for the one we love, let us talk to him in our heart, simply, clearly, and tenderly, imagining that happy moment when we meet again.

Someone we particularly love does not seem to care for us?

Let us, like him/her, say to ourselves that there are millions of unique, and even best persons on this planet. He/She is free to care or not care for us. Let us send him/her our best thoughts, not forgetting to glance at the other persons around.

Are our parents not the way we would like them to be?

Let us say to ourselves that we chose them to help us progress in our life and let us be grateful for everything they gave and still give us.

Do our children seem to forget us?

As the poet Khalil Gibran said in his book "*The prophet*", our children are not ours, they were given to us **to raise them.**

They certainly have other preoccupations than ours but love us more than it seems.

Do we have financial problems?

Life is wealth in itself and we are its heirs. Instead of thinking about what we do not have, let us cool down and think of abundance and prosperity. Let us imagine we live the way we want. It does not mean that we can spend money we do not have. It would be a bad idea. With patience, a lot of confidence, and enough courage, we will get everything we want and even more.

If Heaven could care for flowers and give them beauty and perfume, why wouldn't he do it for us? The only problem is us, with our doubts and lack of confidence in Him and His abundance.

Did we lose our job?

Let our imagination see that we find the perfect job both for us and for the company. And that our employer is as satisfied with us that we are with him, imagining a great and adequate money income.

Did we lose something?

Most of the time, we find it when we stop thinking of it. **I read in K.O. Schmidt's book "*Le hasard n'existe pas*" (*"Chance does not exists"*) that when life takes something from us, it is to grant us with a better gift**. So why regret what we lost? Because it will not help getting it back and moreover something better is expecting us.

Do we have health issues?

As we know, the main issue is not the disease in itself, which is just a "wake up call", asking us to fix our mistakes, but rather our fear of sickness. Paralyzed by fear, we cannot behave as we should, to maintain or come back to a healthy condition. This fear will disappear as soon as we understand its meaning, telling us that this beneficial elimination crisis is meant to maintain or improve our health.

Is our health or that of a dear person compromised?

As long as there is hope, there is life. So, let us enjoy each moment to live better or assist the one who might go. So that he can feel as calm as possible to enter his new dimension. In this new dimension, where, according to Jeanne Morranier and other equally credible authors, all those who have known and loved them on earth are waiting to welcome them in an ineffable love.

Did we lose someone we love?

It is certainly the worse pain we could endure. But if we trust in eternal life, even if we cannot see this person anymore, she is still living next to us. "*We sit in your sofa and sleep in your beds*", can we read in one of the seven books that Jeanne Morranier wrote in automatic writing, under the guidance of her prematurely lost son. Death is a necessary step in the cycle of evolution, like it turns the caterpillar into a butterfly, we must die to be reborn until we reach perfection.

Do we have other problems or many at the same time?

Let's do this: in our heart, our mind or on a piece of paper that we will keep in a diary, a book, or a text-book that we read several times a day, let's write the words that best summarize the situation we are worried about. If it is about illness, let us write "health" and repeat or sing it out on every tune, imagining everything that will come once we recover.

Do we have difficulties making ends meet?

Let's write "abundance" and "prosperity" or a similar word representing the situation that we wish, and ten, a hundred or a thousand times let us relax and breathe deeply and peacefully until our imagination shows us what we will do with the wealth that we need.

Make ours the good habit of only thinking of and talking about what goes well.

It will keep us connected to the highest frequencies and allow us to hear this "little voice" that is always there to guide us for our best. The best to do, every time we are angry, is to go to bed, or even better, fast and purge.

If not, go fishing, running, swimming, painting, gardening, biking, riding a horse, watching a movie or anything that helps us to modify our thoughts.

But do not get it wrong, these things can only be temporary, whatever precious it seems; it will never change the quality of our humors that we have to constantly cleanse and revitalize if we want to "Live Really Alive".

This is why, if we greet each morning as if it were the most beautiful gift and learn to live in the present, we will be surprised by its beauty. It will be easier if we are healthy, a privilege for those who treat themselves as nature has planned. Those who have a "good blood".

Good blood makes good sense.

Good sense always connects us to the highest frequencies. All our doubts, fears and rebellions melt like snow under the sunshine, with love, peace, beauty, joy, harmony, and prosperity that grow in the healthy ground of our garden.

Draw up the balance sheet

Any business necessarily has to draw up the balance sheet and similarly we should evaluate the cost of a painful, sick, and awful life and compare it with the benefits of a healthy life.

I am talking of global health, physical, psychological, or emotional.

These three factors are necessary to create this superior and highly desirable state enjoyed by people with a full, true, and natural health.

A healthy life, to be protected, improved, and developed with a tiny part of the energy and means we use to destroy it.

You do not believe me?

Challenge the cost of these so-called foods which bring no energy but leave an incredible quantity of residues.

Considering the forests that were destroyed to wrap these empty products that advertising forces us to buy.

Count how much alcohol, tobacco and medicines that replace their poisoning and depriving effects, finally cost.

And what about surgery, psychiatric clinics, hospitals, prisons, that result from this absurd way to feed ourselves, and make people sick or pushes them on the wrong path.

Even if medical insurance pays for these treatments, we all pay for it in the end, and the cost is huge. Money cost that could be better used for so many interesting things helping man's happiness and health. One coming with the other, do not forget it.

We can also consider the cost of unemployment, exclusion, and wars, in their financial aspect. And also, the cost of energy wasted in pain, which is priceless. Imagine for a moment that we use these resources to protect, enhance or even recover our most precious asset, rather that spoil it as we do so well.

This true health that makes of our youngsters strong, happy, confident, courageous, imaginative co-creators of the universe, instead of unemployed, excluded, delinquents, junkies, suicidal persons or even gangsters.

This true health that creates happy and responsible women and men, who will become respected, useful, and honored seniors.

A truly healthy condition without which, in one word or in ten, no-one on earth can "Live Really Alive".

Live really alive

So! my younger son will not ever tell me again that my book is like the invisible man, we hear a lot, but never see him.

*Because it is finished,
done, and over!*

I mean, almost... because I still have one or two things to remind you about our body's, this prodigious laboratory for living, functioning.

*Our body, which
it is necessary and
indispensable to consider
and treat as nature intended.*

According to it, we will considerably enhance our health, and least but not last, we will recover our most precious asset:

The cosmic or universal guidance,
or at least, our instinct without
which we cannot walk straight.

Walking against the good sense, the sense of life and all its gifts.

Our instinct, without which we can only access our true wealth in the greatest illusion...

This true wealth which has been replaced by power and money...

Money which, if it's necessary, and sometimes indispensable in the world that we created, cannot buy what is essential!

If money can buy a house **It does not buy a home**

If it buys ***entertainment and pleasure*** It does not buy **happiness**

If it buys ***sex*** It does not buy **love**

If it buys ***education*** It does not buy **knowledge**

If it buys ***a lawsuit*** It does not buy **justice**

If it buys ***medical drugs*** It does not buy **health**

Real health cannot be bought,

but we can protect, maintain, or repair it

with what nature provided for us.

Here are Steve Job's last words:

"*I have reached the top in business*" did he say. "*For everyone, my life is a success. Though I do not have that much pleasure but at work. After all, wealth is only a fact that I have got used to. Right now, I am lying sick in a bed and I realize that all this wealth that I have been quite proud of, has lost its taste and brightness now that I am facing my own death.*

I cannot take all this wealth with me."

It means that, what is important is not to have as much money as possible, but to have as much as we need to live at our best. One being compatible with the other. But the first and real wealth is to be healthy, connected to the universal intelligence in charge of guiding us throughout life, for ours and everyone's best, as life intelligence always does.

Even if sometimes life shakes and hurts us, to take us to our real destination.

As it happened to me: I should have continued my medical studies, to heal, as I always wanted to. But the essay to pass the 6th grade's exam showed my real destiny:

The subject was: "One day you will be an adult and chose a profession". Which one and why?

As if it were automatic-writing, I wrote:

"I do not want to have a profession, I want to be a woman, I want to love, I want to care and heal..."

Without interruption I filled up two pages. I was supposed to go, the following year, to high school in Epinal (the main city in the area), and rejoiced. But the last school day my mother went to the doctor's who told her:

"***Absolute rest and lots of food Mrs Kiesel***"

For the first time, that day she waited for me after class and told the teacher that I would not go to high school. Since I was the eldest of five children, I should remain at the village's school to help her.

I was so despaired that I cried all the tears I had, and so did the teacher, repeating:

"***No, not her, this is impossible, it is so unfair!***"

Yes, that's how things happened.

Even after she perfectly followed three years of medical treatments, my mother left us weighing only 55 pounds (25 kg).

50 pounds of terrible suffering

For most French people in 1942, there were restrictions, but we had a garden and a field to gather fruit. We also bred rabbits, hens a pig and a goat and dad, besides his work, could also catch wild rabbits that he traded for sugar, meat, butter, and bread tickets at the Prefecture of Epinal.

Mum did not lack of food at all,

it was the opposite, knowing what I know now, she was rather wrongly and over fed.

This caused her a severe constipation. Her belly was so dilated that I thought we were going to have another baby, sister, or brother.

Since she could not eliminate, she was nit hungry and refused all the food I brought her; smearing my face with it if I insisted too much. At least, it made her laugh while, crying, I went back to the kitchen, wondering what I could do to make her eat.

Every two days, when the doctor came for his visit, he kept on repeating that she had to eat to recover. A Doctor's saying was sacred, so I blindly obeyed.

Even if, each time I could make her eat, she writhed in pain. So, I called the doctor who gave another drug and repeated that she absolutely had to eat to get better.

As a result, feeding her as we did and considering that she could not eliminate, we practically pushed her into the graveyard.

I was 16 years old and became the substitute mother for my four brothers and sisters, responsible for the household. The bright side of the story, in hard times there is always one, is that, instead of studying to become a doctor like any other, I discovered what allowed me to do what I was meant for

Love, care and heal!

I learnt from life how to live a happy and healthy life, rather than fill up hospitals, prisons, psychiatry rooms, lawyers' appointments, or the employment office.

Even if it is true to say that we choose with love and have ideas and thoughts to create our life; we absolutely need our body's cells to love and think.

This is why it is quite normal to treat them as nature planned.

Simple good sense!

Both the way they work, and their liquids' quality are crucial for our state of consciousness' level, feelings, acts and ideas.

During a period, I received up to 20 unemployed patients. One year and a half after, without any other change than clean their "humors" with the right food.

All had found a better job than the one they had previously lost.

Was it by chance? I do not think so, because by giving their body the energy required for their cells, they managed to get off the fears in which their toxemia had locked them. Then they were able to connect to higher frequencies and therefore imagine, believe, and attract the situation that they wished.

There is no miracle, everything has an explanation because life obeys to principles, rules, and laws, whatever we call them, and respecting them is simply logical.

Our difficulties, pains, and diseases, before all and despite appearances, all come from our behavioral mistakes, themselves issued by food poisoning and deficiencies.

It is not through fighting but by modifying what caused them, that we will free ourselves.

Similarly, fighting and battling against cancer or any other disease will not stop them.

But it will rather be **by oxygenating and feeding our cells and by cleaning their surrounding liquids.**

A great and ultimate truth being that, if my mother had not died, I would never have learnt what life and health are by following a medical course (which would have taught me many other interesting things though) because this is not what they teach at Medical University.

This is the reason why, before I finish this book, I want to remind you some facts meant to enlighten you.

You probably know someone having frequent colds, bronchitis, asthma, or other respiratory conditions. Take a look at what they usually eat and what they prefer and cannot stop eating.

Isn't it mostly bread, pasta, rice, pizzas, potatoes, cookies candies and starches?

If not, I would be rather surprised...

You will probably also notice that they are imprisoned in their fears and also lack of energy and self-confidence. To address these awful deficiencies, they stuff with their favorite stimulant foods like sugar, chocolate, coffee, tea, and soda.

In opposite to common belief, slow carbs cannot provide the energy that they do not possess. And those who are eating them, have to compensate with an over consumption of stimulants:

Like strong coffee, Italians love with their pasta

Or tea, Asians drink with rice

Coffee and Rum with chili for South Americans

Bier and coffee for Belgians who eat a lot of French fries

And coke with hamburgers for Northern Americans

When, by simply eating the sugar of life you will not need those anymore.

You may also notice that asthma, which did not exist before, has recently developed with the consumption of slow carbs, which are moreover cheap and easy to cook and that our kids love when they eat pasta.

This terrible trap led to an amount of 8% adults, 6 to 10% children and 10 to 18% teenagers suffering from asthma.

And this is not considering all the allergies, sterile women, unemployed persons, and people with AIDS.

Talking about the ones who love meat and cannot live without, you will probably see them drinking wine, beer, or other alcohols, and see that they are generally in pain, irascible and violent.

Did you ever wonder why youngsters always want to have fun?

Because eating this food, they lost this natural happiness that their forefathers had thanks to a healthy food. So, they replace it with alcohol that their cells demand because it brings a momentary illusion of having fun, something that stimulants do so well.

I remember that day when I was invited for a conference in their city's medical university. I was surprised to see, written on top of these students to do list, the word alcohol with an "s" and written in bold characters.

They were strong and beautiful young persons and one of them was a gymnastic teacher, so I told them how surprised I was. They answered that, to have fun, they definitely needed alcohol.

Of course, after fun time came sad time,

After stimulation came depression,

And if they do not change these habits, we know what will become of them...

This need for stimulants is stronger as their food is dead and cooked and cannot provide the energy they need. If the first place they really think that they need alcohol, which will soon make them addicted to drugs or medicines, something that youngsters correctly fed will never ever need.

The correct way of feeding has nothing to do with meat for proteins, milk and dairy products or cheese for calcium, slow carbs for glucose, as the money driven science and medicine taught us since the last world war.

Chemical molecules do not only destroy our planet but also constitute the main components of the new drugs that we consequently more and more often take.

Let us remember that before these days, there were few drug companies, but within three quarters of a century they have become the world's biggest trust.

This is quite easy to understand once we know that this over exciting and dead food can only connect us to the universe's lowest frequencies. Pretending to heal, each time it tries, we stop our body's attempts to eliminate, and keep its overloads deep inside. Where they will turn into always more serious and frequent illnesses.

One cancer out of three, a famous oncologist recently told me...

Diabetes, cardiovascular strokes, Alzheimer's, Parkinson's, multiple sclerosis and suicidal or murderous ideas have been developing like never before.

Is this what we expected from progress?
Of course not!

If we had understood and treated them the right way, our cells would have connected to the highest frequencies, leading us to a healthy mental, psychological, and physical life.

Considering that the same laws rule what is small and what is big, if our body is made of billions of little cells, could each one of us perhaps be a cell of the universe?

This Uni-verse from
which the words "UNI"
and "United" comes.

It could mean that each one of us being both one and unique, like that of our body's cells, our role could be to be connected and participate to the life of the whole.

It could also mean that none of us is more important than the other and should dominate or be dominated. This would turn the domination laws into sharing, for the sake of this Universe that we all desire.

That sounds rather
utopian, I know.

Unless, I repeat it, we accept, like our body's cells do, that our real goal on Earth is

to act one with the other,

and one for the other,

for the best of the whole,

as well as ours.

We would certainly be happier and more confident that way than working only for our own sake.

This is a natural law that **as long as the spring gives water, it receives more; and once it stops giving, it dries.**

In other words, to receive the true gifts of Life, we must give the best of ourselves.

So, give, let us give our best.

If we treat our body, this fantastic laboratory for life, well enough, it will be easy, because it is the most precious of laboratories indeed...

This way we will fly over the clouds, remaining under the sun rays where the solution for all our problems lays. Because we receive d from nature everything to make of our lives and of the earth a paradise of health and well-being, searching for it everywhere when it is here at our feet.

Because life is simple!

So simple, that we hardly understand how people thought that we could heal with dead animals and poisons, that certainly will project any healthy person to sickness.

But we did it and still do, whereas nature gave us all we need to protect, improve, and even recover our most precious asset.

That is to say true health, the only one that can make us happy and make of Earth a paradise.

The earthly paradise, because if hell is here, as my grand ma used to say, paradise is here too!

Paradise can only be rooted in a garden.

A wonderful garden that provides us with seeds, plants, fruits, and vegetables, if we know how to grow them, giving us all the energy that they received from air, soil, water, and sun.

Nothing but this energy can connect us to the Universe's High Frequencies intended to offer us this paradisiac bunch of flowers made of health, joy, love, faith, courage, beauty, goodness, creativity, abundance, and happiness.

That is meant for all its creatures who live according to the laws, rules, and principles that Nature decided for their best functioning.

Rules, laws, or principles, call them as you want, but hurry to find them and enter this amazing garden, the Garden of Eden, where your poor supplications and lamentations will become alleluias of grace and gratitude.

Recommended readings

Books in French and English

- "The China Study" by T. Colin Campbell & Thomas M. Campbell
- "Sugar Blues" by William Dufty
- "Medical Mafia" by Lanctot Ghislaine Staff
- "The Essene of the Gospel of Peace, the Aramaic and Old Slavonic Texts Compared", Edited and Translated By Edmond Bordeaux Szekely
- "The Little Prince" by Antoine de Saint-Exupery
- "The Amazing Liver and Gallbladder Flush" by Andreas Moritz
- "Edgar Cayce: Encyclopedia Healing" by Edgar Cayce
- "Conversations with God, Book 4: Awaken the Species, A New and Unexpected Dialogue" by Neale Donald Walsch
- "The Four Agreements" Toltec Wisdom Collection by Don Miguel Ruiz

- "The Cosmic Ordering Service" by Barbel Mohr
- "Synchrodestiny: Discover the Power of Meaningful Coincidence to Manifest Abundance in Your Life" by Deepak Chopra and Nightingale-Conant
- "Sprouts the miracle food" *by Steve Meyerowitz - The sproutman - www.Sproutman.com*

Books in French:

- "Sois Malade Et Tais-Toi !" Jean-Jacques Rocca - "Stay sick and keep silent" or "Sick and silent"
- "VACCINATION: erreur médicale du SIÈCLE: dangers et conséquences" Dr Louis de Brouwer - "Vaccination: The worst error of the century: dangers and outcome"
- "Médecins du ciel, médecins de la Terre" Maguy Lebrun - "Heavenly healers, and doctors from earth"
- "La santé confisquée" Monique et Mirko Beljanski - "They stole our health" or "Our health's hijacking"
- "Découvertes interdites, l'affaire Beljanski René Bickel - "The Bejanski case" (how lobbies silenced extraordinary recoveries)
- "La vaccination, cette grande illusion" René Bickel - "Vaccination: the Great Illusion: Humorous and Informative, bringing awareness and critical thinking about vaccinations."
- "Secrets et Sagesse du Corps (Médecine des profondeurs)" Dr A. Salmanoff. "Secrets and body wisdom" (a medicine of the depths)
- "Le Grand Livre de l'Aromathérapie" Nelly Grosjean - "A complete guide of aromatherapy" or "A complete guide of essential oils"

- "Les Cures de sudation et autres moyens naturels d'élimination par la peau" Pierre Valentin Marchesseau – "Sweating and other natural skin elimination techniques"
- "Les cures d'eau du Curé Kneipp" Pierre Valentin Marchesseau – "Hydrotherapy, the techniques of Father Kneipp"
- "La Révolution de la Pensée Intégrale" Patrick Drouot – "The revolution of holistic thinking"
- "Manger 'SOLEIL' - des recettes de graines germées et de jeunes pousses" Marcel Monnier – "Eat with the sun" – recipes with sprouts and germinated seeds
- "Les graines germées – livre de cultures" Marcel Monnier – "How to grow sprouts"
- "SAUVEZ VOTRE CORPS" Dr Catherine Kousmine – "Save your body"
- "Le livre du Bonheur" Marcelle Auclair – "The book of happiness"
- "La Bouffe ou la Vie" Dr Yves Vivini – "Grub or life"
- "L'Homme, cet inconnu" Dr Alexis Carrel. "Man, this unknown creature" or "Unknown mankind"
- "Le Hasard n'existe pas" de Karl Otto Schmidt – "chance doesn't exist"
- "Le retour à la Santé par le Jeûne" Dr Edmond Bertholet – "The healing power of fasting"
- "La Guerre du Cru" Guy-Claude Burger – "fighting for raw food"
- "La Nouvelle Science de Guérir" Dr Louis Khune – "The new science of healing"
- "Abusez des Vitamines" Dr Linus Pauling – "Over-use vitamins"

- "Femmes, si vous saviez" Pr Henri Joyeux – "Women should know" (from puberty to menopause)
- "Le lait : une sacrée vacherie ?" Nicolas Le Berre – "Nasty milk ?
- "L'INSTANT CRU" Marie Sophie L. – "Time for raw food" raw vegan recipes without starch
- "LA CURE ZEN DETOX AROMATIC" tomes 1 et 2, Nelly Grosjean – "The Zen Detox Aromatic Diet"

I thank all the persons who granted us the opportunity to be informed and helped us choose a true, total and natural health: Knapp, Geoffroy, Monod, Carton, Shelton, Solomidès, Lagarde, Dunville, Rouhet, Walford, Atkins, Nieper, Delbet, Pfeiffer, Lesser, Laborit, Shute, Kaufman, Hoffer…

The Publishers

Biovie is a home-made, engaged, activist publishing company releasing books in the fields of organic living food as well as of parenthood. We especially published the first book of raw recipes in France *Healthful Cuisine*, together with *The Detox Miracle Sourcebook* of Doctor Robert Morse.

Biovie works in the areas of practical ecology since 2007. Its particularity is to offer high-quality organic products, uncommon or even unknown on the French market. We ideally choose big packagings, opting for bulk and non transformed, raw products. Our distribution channels are the shortest possible.

Among the ones recommended by Irène Grosjean, you will find, round our way, fresh algae from Brittany, dehydrated algae at low temperature, numerous varieties of sprouted seeds, automatic sprouters and a Japanese water filtering and dynamization system.

We also offer tigernuts to make milks and economical and nutritional plant-based mixes, spirulina and chlorella in bulk, fresh klamath alga, barley grass juice, cold-dehydrated durian, marine plasma in bulk, ghassoul, high-quality clays, unique plates in olive wood.

Recently, we offer an online support to learn living food with the family, including innovative, quick recipes, to make with kids, and with low-cost and easy-to-find ingredients, as well as live "batchcooking" classes from our kitchen to prepare raw meals for the whole week in two hours.

Practicing this type of diet daily since more than 15 years, it seemed to us important to pass down our recipes and skills for a simple and inexpensive cuisine. Thank you for your trust in our business!

To be informed of our news, new products and special offers, leave us your email at:

mailchi.mp/biovie/actus

Aurélie and Eric Viard

www.biovie.fr

Notes

Pierre-Valentin Marchesseau was a biologist. He is considered the father of French naturopathy, for having imported and translated the concepts in 1935.In 1973, he created in Paris the "Institut d'Hygiène Vitale" where he trained many naturopaths. He self-publishes about fifty books in which he gives his knowledge in naturopathy and which were used during his trainings.

Knock or Dr.Knock
"Knock or the triumph or Medicine" is a play by Jules Romains, ..., a squeaky comedy, Knock denounced manipulation, whether of medicine or any ideology, as well as of any business. The play has remained famous, among other things, for Dr. Knock's maxim: "*Every healthy person is a sick person who ignores himself.*"

Jeanne Calment

Jeanne Calment is a French supercentenary born on 21 February 1875 in Arles (Bouches-du-Rhône) and died in the same city on 4 August 1997, at the age of one hundred and twenty-two years, five months, and fourteen days. ... she became the longest living human being among those whose date of birth has been verified.

From Wikipedia, consulted on 22/08/2020

Printed in Dunstable, United Kingdom

81148545R00198